A Pineapple Republic – A Concise History of Pineapple in Hawaii

David Oglesby and

Joy Ogawa

Zyaoi Media Books

Zyaoi Media Books

Published by Zyaoi Media

Honolulu, Hawaii, U.S.A.

First published in the United States of America by Zyaoi Media

ISBN: 9798697497593

CIP data available

Printed in United States of America

Designed by David Oglesby

Cover Design & Photo by David Oglesby

Dedication Page

To my mother who always supported my projects, to my wife and son who support me now, to my family who taught and loved me along the way; to the Native Hawaiians who made an outstanding civilization and those today who work toward a greater community in the islands and around the world.

– David A. Oglesby

To my bachan (grandmother), Shina Ikeuchi, who bravely emigrated from Toyama, Japan as a picture bride on the last ship in 1924 to marry my gichan (grandfather), Chotaro Hane, a Timekeeper, on the Waialua Pineapple Plantation, now known as Dole Plantation. To my parents for nurturing a storyteller. To my collaborator for championing the humble fruit into a passion project and giving voice to this important and personal story. To all the immigrant groups that made the most of their plantation experience by planting roots in the islands that made modern Hawaii life possible for their children and grandchildren.

~ Joy Ogawa

Table of Contents

Preface

Whereas, without the active support and intervention by the United States diplomatic and military representatives, the insurrection against the Government of Queen Liliuokalani would have failed for lack of popular support and insufficient arms.

Whereas, in a message to Congress on December 18, 1893, President Grover Cleveland reported fully and accurately on the illegal acts of the conspirators, described such acts as an "act of war, committed with the participation of a diplomatic representative of the United States and without authority of Congress", and acknowledged that by such acts the government of a peaceful and friendly people was overthrown... President Cleveland further concluded that a "substantial wrong has thus been done which a due regard for our national character as well as the rights of the injured people requires we should endeavor to repair" and called for the restoration of the Hawaiian monarchy.

Whereas, the indigenous Hawaiian people never directly relinquished their claims to their inherent sovereignty as a people or over their national lands to the United States, either through their monarchy or through a plebiscite or referendum.

Whereas, the health and well-being of the Native Hawaiian people is intrinsically tied to their deep feelings and attachment to the land;

Whereas, the long-range economic and social changes in Hawaii over the nineteenth and early twentieth centuries have been devastating to the population and to the health and well-being of the Hawaiian people;

Whereas, the Native Hawaiian people are determined to preserve, develop and transmit to future generations their ancestral territory, and their cultural identity in accordance with their own spiritual and traditional beliefs, customs, practices, language, and social institutions,

Now, therefore, be it
Resolved by the Senate and House of Representatives of the United States of America in Congress assembled,

The Congress
- apologizes to Native Hawaiians on behalf of the people of the United States for the overthrow of the Kingdom of Hawaii on January 17, 1893... and the deprivation of the rights of Native Hawaiians to self-determination.

- expresses its commitment to acknowledge the ramifications of the overthrow of the Kingdom of Hawaii, in order to provide a proper foundation for reconciliation between the United States and the Native Hawaiian people; and

- urges the President of the United States to also acknowledge the ramifications of the overthrow of the Kingdom of Hawaii and to support reconciliation efforts between the United States and the Native Hawaiian people.

Excerpts from Public Law 103-150, the "Apology Resolution" to Native Hawaiians, on November 23, 1993 - acknowledges the 100th anniversary of the January 17, 1893 overthrow of the Kingdom of Hawaii.

Introduction

Come to Hawaii! The sun shines bright, the beaches are inviting, and the pineapple fields stretch as far as the eye can see. There's plenty to do and plenty to see. Everyone's happy, and you're welcomed upon arrival. Who knows, maybe you'll find an opportunity and stay. Or at least say I've seen it. Yes, life in Hawaii is good... it's paradise on earth.

That's what the marketing tells ya, anyway. Because they're selling an image. And boy, does it sell... Yep, you'd think this place was the Garden of Eden!

Like the movie, L.A. Confidential expressed, the image usually tells only part of the story. Hollywood did that for L.A., and the pineapple arguably did the same for Hawaii. And like Hollywood, the pineapple industry did help influence and shape many things beyond the image we see.

This book deals with the people and actions that developed the industry and the islands into what we see today. First a brief history of first contacts between Hawaiians and the outside world. Then a look at how the pineapple industry developed with highlights on major contributors. Next, a look at the people who came to work the fields and the canneries. Finally, a glance at the rise and fall of pineapples in Hawaii and how the industry helped develop modern-day Hawaii.

Chapter 1

In the Beginning

In the central Pacific, on a chain of islands known as - Hawaii, in the high plains of an island called - Oahu sits one of the last remnants of the pineapple industry in the islands. This industry and people were key to the shaping of this archipelago. Culture, politics, economics, and notoriety changed and grew on the back of this product. A product so expensive before Hawaiian cultivation, which few knew or used it. This is the story of pineapple and how it's shaped Hawaii.

For most of the 20th-century, pineapples' association with Hawaii added to its majesty, and Hawaii's majesty also grew from that association. Pineapple derives from South America, and until the voyage of Columbus, Europe had no idea of its existence. When the pineapple first arrived in Hawaii is unknown, but its presence was first recorded in 1813. Don Francisco de Paula y Marin, a Spanish advisor to King Kamehameha I, was the first to cultivate pineapples in the islands along with introducing many other species of plants.

Don Francisco was born in the Andalusian (southernmost) region of Spain in 1774. Little is known about his first years in Hawaii, but he settled on Oahu with a small group of foreigners near the turn of the 19th century. At some point, he learned the language, married multiple women, and won favor with the King. He would soon become an advisor, interpreter, and part-time physician for the royal court. His main contribution to the history of the islands lies in his love and propagation of many plants. Besides pineapples, Marin is believed to have introduced olives, grapes, coffee, tamarind, and possibly tobacco to Hawaii. Having been gifted a sizable plot of land in downtown Oahu close to the King's quarters, many of his plantings would help his own business enterprises as he was one of the first significant suppliers of provisions and quarters for ships visiting the islands.

The pineapples Marin is given credit for are by far the most important product he promoted during his life. This introduction became one of the dominant industries and defined the fabric of Hawaii in under a century. For this to happen, many events occurred – events that fueled change, and that change fueled the growth of the fruit.

Hawaii is a derivative of the Hawaiian word "Owhyhee," meaning homeland. And this homeland; these islands and their people suffered greatly since the arrival of Captain James Cook in 1778. In 1795 Kamehameha I conquered and united the Hawaiian Islands. He may have thought that by uniting the islands, he could protect his people from outside influences.

Regardless of his reasons, his Kingdom, these islands in the middle of the Pacific, would be conquered in less than a century. Later and subsequent leaders would promote changes for better or worse. These have shaped Hawaii into what we know today. One of the systems that helped the pineapple industry had its first seeds planted in another sector – sugar.

Sugar introduced the plantation system, and that system changed Hawaii forever. Sugar was not new to the islands - Hawaiians had cultivated the plant long before Europeans arrived. Still, once these recent immigrants started to grow it as a cash crop, it became extremely successful. The first successful sugar cane plantation was launched in 1835 by Ladd and Company at Koloa, Kauai.

In 1833, William Ladd, along with his partners, Peter Allen Brinsmade, and William Northey Hooper started a store and wharf located in downtown Honolulu. Two years later, they leased some 980 acres of land from the Royal Governor of Kauai - Kaikioʻewa. Hooper. One of the partners, would eventually move to Kauai and become the manager of operations and begin the system that would remain in place in one form or another until the present day. The initial labor force on this plantation consisted of twenty-five laborers of native Hawaiian descent and several overseers of European descent. Hooper provided payments in a script that could be redeemed for food and supplies at the plantation store. With this, Hooper had effectively started a plantation system that would be the basis for future sugar and pineapple farms throughout Hawaii. A system that not only introduced technological advancements to the islands, but a hierarchical system based on ethnicity that encouraged the suppression of non-European populations for decades.

(Ladd and Company, Kauai - Hawaii State Archives)

As the sugar business grew, more prosperous and influential, a gradual shift in politics began to take hold. Foreigners started demanding, persuading, and finally purchasing large amounts of property. Hawaiians were more communal when it came to land ownership. This change, however, started to alter the political landscape as foreigners began coming in increasing numbers. And as they occupied more land, they wanted more to say over the laws that governed the islands. As these sugar barons' investments grew – stakes rose, and the prospects of letting those in power control them became untenable. It was so much so that in 1887, these men acting under the name, The Honolulu Rifle Company militia, forced the then reigning King - Kalākaua to sign over most of his rights under the so-called Bayonet Constitution. A constitution that gave more authority and rights to this new planter's class who had secured a stronghold over the economy. Under this new structure, it was not only the monarchy suppressed but also the voice of the Native Hawaiians who had seen little to no benefit from the changes in

3

progress. Three years later, in 1890, the United States signed the McKinley Tariff into law, a law that sharply raised tariffs and effectively ended a period of Hawaiian dominance over the sugar industry in North America.

The Reciprocity Treaty of 1875 had been negotiated over several decades by those who primarily grew sugar. Planters had been hampered by taxes imposed on Hawaiian goods, and this agreement had benefited them the most. In 1890 as the McKinley Tariff reinstated restrictions on trade, the fall of sugar pushed Hawaii into economic turmoil. The planters who had enjoyed years of favorable laws with the United States were now subject to higher costs and more competition from other foreign producers.

The dependence on sugar and the individuals who ran the industry was surely weighing on Queen Lili'uokalani's mind when she proposed a new constitution in 1893 to replace the 1887 version signed under duress by her brother. Her new version, if ratified, would revoke many of the powers accumulated by this plantation class and put the Queen squarely back in control of the Kingdom. Although opposed in effect to the entirety of this document, the primary areas of contention for foreign-born and recent generation residents who were the following – nobles or individuals in the upper house of the legislature – would return to being appointed by the Queen instead of elected. - Property requirements for voters would be decreased, thus allowing a greater number of citizens to vote - The Queen would again be responsible for the appointment of governors to each island for four years. - American and European residents who were granted suffrage in 1887 would lose the right to vote, and Article 78 of the 1887 Constitution required the monarch to perform "with the advice and consent of the Cabinet" was left out.

These proposals were met with massive support by the populace, a majority of which were still of Native Hawaiian heritage; however, as could be expected, the Americans and foreign nationals who were around forty-six percent of the total population were in strong opposition. Hoping for American intervention, the plantation class began planning a coup.

On January 16th, 1893, a letter was signed and sent to John L. Stevens, the U.S. minister to Hawaii stating, "Sir, We, the undersigned, citizens and residents of Honolulu, respectfully represent that, in view of recent public events in this Kingdom, culminating in the revolutionary acts of Queen Liliuokalani on Saturday 'last, the public safety is menaced and lives and property are in peril, and we appeal to you and the United States forces at your command for assistance. The Queen, with the aid of armed force and accompanied by threats of violence and bloodshed from those with whom she was acting, attempted to proclaim a new constitution; and, while prevented for the time from accomplishing her object, declared publicly that she would only defer her action. This conduct and action was upon occasion and under circumstances which we created general alarm and terror. We are unable to protect ourselves without aid, and, therefore, pray for the protection of the United States forces. Signed Citizen's Committee of Safety."

Having declared their fears; they acted the following day, January 17th, 1893. Queen Liliuokalani, who had seen in her lifetime the erosion of power held by the Ali'i - the royal class of Hawaii - along with the diminished power of her people, brought forth an ultimate conclusion when her power to rule was utterly stripped and given to the insurgent sugar plantation owners. Owners who were descendants of mostly missionary families which had come to Hawaii to aid and enlighten a so-called heathen and ignorant local populace. Within her lifetime, most of the changes that lead to this day had occurred – in around half a century, maybe 2 or 3 generations removed from her birth the Hawaiians had lost control of their land.

(Queen Liliuokalani - Hawaii State Archives)

Chapter 2

Overthrow

THE "CRIMES I AM CHARGED WITHAL" The three " intolerable " measures with which my government stands charged by those who succeeded in enlisting the aid of so powerful an ally as the United States in this revolution are as follows: — First, — That I proposed to promulgate a new constitution. I have already shown that two-thirds of my people declared their dissatisfaction with the old one; as well they might, for it was a document originally designed for a republic, hastily altered when the conspirators found that they had not the courage to assassinate the King. It is alleged that my proposed constitution was to make such changes as to give to the sovereign more power, and to the cabinet or legislature less, and that only subjects, in distinction from temporary residents, could exercise suffrage. In other words, that I was to restore some of the ancient rights of my people. I had listened to whatever had been advised, had examined whatever drafts of constitutions others had brought me, and promised but little. But, supposing I had thought it wise to limit the exercise of suffrage to those who owed allegiance to no other country; is that different from the usage in all other civilized nations on earth? Is there another country where a man would be allowed to vote, to seek for office, to hold the most responsible of positions, without becoming naturalized, and reserving to himself the privilege of protection under the guns of a foreign man-of-war at any moment when he should quarrel with the government under which he lived? Yet this is exactly what the quasi Americans, who call themselves Hawaiians now and Americans when it suits them, claimed the right to do at Honolulu. - Hawaii's Story by Hawaii's Queen - Queen Liliuokalani -

The Citizen's Committee of Safety effectively took control of one government building to bolster claims of authority. At that time, U.S. Minister Stevens acted upon the letter he had received and indeed ordered the landing of 162 sailors and Marines from aboard the USS

Boston.

Their march from landing on Hawaiian soil to positions was rather quick, as the Boston was docked in Honolulu Harbor only a few blocks from central Honolulu and the Palace. Around 5 pm they took positions at the U.S. Embassy, the Consulate Office, and Arlington Hotel. All of these buildings were within minutes of the Palace and made Queen Liliuokalani readily aware of the formable threat to her Kingdom and rule. Queen Liliuokalani and her loyal representatives made attempts to receive support from foreign emissaries. However, every government with a diplomatic presence in Hawaii, except for the United Kingdom, recognized the insurgents as the rightful leaders within 48 hours of the overthrow.

These countries included Chile, Austria-Hungary, Mexico, Russia, the Netherlands, Imperial Germany, Sweden, Spain, Imperial Japan, Italy, Portugal, Denmark, Belgium, China, Peru, and France.

Queen Liliuokalani having had warm relations with Great Britain and Queen Victoria in particular, expected British support against this attack on her sovereignty. She had met and attended Queen Victoria's Golden Jubilee in England and was received warmly along with other Hawaiian dignitaries during her stay. To her surprise and disbelief, Great Britain, a revered ally, essentially stayed silent and offered zero support to for the Queen's cause. This put a final chapter on the rule of Hawaii by the ancestors of those who first inhabited these islands between 700 to 1500 years prior.

From that point to the present, Hawaii would continue to change rapidly. These changes in politics, culture, and economics were a far cry from what Hawaiians of only a few generations earlier would have imagined. And the plantation system and pineapple industry would be vital in the shaping of Hawaii's future.

On the day of the overthrow, a foundation was laid for the impact the pineapple industry would make on this land. Although he would not become the official leader of the Republic of Hawaii till July 4th of the following year, Sanford Ballard Dole had been a leader in circles that had pushed for power.

His influence had guided many of the provisions drafted into the 1887 Constitution of the Kingdom of Hawaii, and the letter of January 16th by the Committee of Safety as such Dole was chosen and became the 1st Territorial Governor of Hawaii and first head of state of non-native ancestry. His cousin James, known as the "Pineapple King," would come later and receive more notoriety, but Governor Dole's influence and leadership laid the foundation on which his cousin would prosper.

Sanford's parents were American missionaries originally from Maine. In 1841, his father and mother were the initial teachers at Punahou, and as soon as the school increased in numbers, his father became principal. Sanford was born in 1844, and his mother died days after his birth. He was raised by Hawaiians and his stepmother, Charlotte Close Knapp. At the age of eleven, he moved with his parents to Kōloa, Kaua'i where his father helped start another boarding school.

Sanford would eventually return to Oahu to finish school at Punahou before heading to the east coast of America, where he attended Williams College (1866-67). There he studied religion then law; however, he never formally attended law school. In 1868 Dole returned to Hawaii and started to practice law. As his practice grew, he became more familiar and connected with leaders in the Hawaiian community. Through these friendships, Dole gained his first government appointment as Commissioner of Private Ways and Water for the district of Kona in 1873. By 1884, he won election to the Hawaiian legislature as a representative and reelection in 1886. The following year vaulted his presence in island politics as he was a significant contributor to the Bayonet Constitution that restricted the power of the monarchy.

Through his involvement in the constitutional revolt, the King's cabinet appointed Dole to the Supreme Court as an Associate Justice in the same year (1887). An appointment King Kalākaua would have inevitably opposed if given the ability. From this position, his involvement in policies within the Kingdom only grew, and he, along with Lorrin A. Thurston, became the primary legal minds behind the rebellion that would eventually lead to the overthrow of

Queen Lili'uokalani.

(Sanford Ballard Dole - Hawaii State Archives)

Chapter 3

Slips Planted

One of Governor Dole's contemporaries, also involved with politics, helped influence the trajectory which the pineapple industry would take. This pioneer arguably played the most crucial role in the industry's development as he laid its groundwork - his name was John Kidwell. John was born in the Southeast of England in a town called Marwood on January 7th, 1849. Around the age of 30, he had managed to find his way to San Francisco. Once there, Kidwell started a career in horticulture. Since the age of fifteen, he had worked with plants and that familiarity led to quick work. Soon he was hired at a well-established nursery run by John Sievers and started to meet many customers from Hawaii. Through these connections, he was informed of the need for a good nursery in the islands, and after gaining letters of introduction, he found his way to Honolulu. Once there, he established his first nursery in 1882.

By the time of his arrival, the Hawaiian Islands that had previously been dominated by native Hawaiian subsistence driven agriculture was well into a period of commercial agriculture that was being driven by sugar cane production. Kidwell knew of demand for pineapple in San Francisco and the poor quality of shipments received from the islands. Up to that point, pineapples were not indeed a commercial business as they were primarily picked wild on the Big Island of Hawaii and then transported to Honolulu. A process that could take a week or more from harvest to transport. In Honolulu, the shipment would be placed on commercial liners to San Francisco. With an average sailing time of 20 days between the Port of Honolulu and San Francisco and the overall poor quality of the fruit that eventually arrived on the west coast of the United States was less than desirable. Kidwell, along with a commercial shipper of fruit named Charles Hensen, decided to attempt to cut the time of transport and improve the quality by growing pineapple in the Manoa Valley on Oahu in 1885. They used wild cuttings from the Big

Island of Hawaii and were successful in cultivating a crop. Unfortunately, the quality of the product remained the same. Later that year, Kidwell decided to send off for another variety of pineapple called the Smooth Cayenne. After testing it by growing a dozen plants, he felt it would be a more successful variety and ordered an additional thousand from Jamaica.

(John Kidwell - Hawaii State Archives)

Out of these plants, six hundred grew very well; still, he was not satisfied, so he sent off to get 31 more varieties to test. After this extended testing, he decided his first choice was the best and scaled up his planting of the Smooth Cayenne variety. He is credited as being one of the first to use stumps of his plantings on a large scale to grow new plants. An idea still in use today. Unfortunately, his first partner Charles Hensen died soon after their partnership began, and he had to carry on alone. This was not to his favor, as Kidwell's expertise was in the growth of the product, not the marketing of it. Regardless, from 1886 to 1899, Kidwell did reasonably well but never great. He sold most of his crops locally with the surplus going to California, although shipping time still presented many problems.

These continuing shipping issues helped produce the next significant development in Hawaiian pineapple production – canning. Kidwell teamed up with a popular hardware salesman, John Emmeluth, to find a way of canning a quality pineapple. After three years of research and development, they landed on a good canning process; unfortunately, by this time, the U.S. had a tariff (McKinley Tariff, 1890) in place on goods from Hawaii, which made it highly unprofitable for them to sell their product. Soon even selling the fresh fruit abroad grew difficult, so Kidwell contracted with a wholesaler to deliver his product.

This also eventually turned out to be as disastrous as his previous calculations. His wholesaler, Peter Camarinos – who soon played a more prominent role in the pineapple industry, sued him for breach of contract. Kidwell had contracted to sell his whole crop of pineapples to Camarinos in December 1888. The contract had been renewed twice. In April 1890, Kidwell had signed a new contract to supply all his output of pineapples that were over three pounds, for which Camarinos agreed to pay thirty-five cents each, for a term of thirty months. In June 1891, Camarinos refused to receive any more pineapples from Kidwell. His claim - Kidwell had sold him poisonous pineapples that were unsalable. Camarinos's brother, who owned a commission house in San Francisco, alleged that Kidwell had written him a letter saying, "he had doctored the pineapples for the sake of killing the growth to prevent persons who bought them from planting the growth, and themselves raising sugarloaf pineapples in the future." While the lawsuit was still in litigation, Camarinos, with the help of his brother and local businessman, George Lycurgus, developed a pineapple plantation in the Kalihi area. By August 1891, they had also established the Pearl City Fruit Company, Ltd., with $23,000 of capital.

Peter Camarinos was originally from Northern Greece. He arrived in Hawaii via San Francisco, where he moved to join his brother Demetrios who had formed a profitable fruit import business. They decided to expand operations to Hawaii, and at twenty-two (1884), Peter traveled to Hawaii to set up a shop. The Camarinos brother's business named the California Fruit Market, became stronger and stronger with this dual representation within the Pacific region. So much so that by March of 1890, Demetrios Camarinos purchased the Emerson, Butler, and Co. Fruit Company. This company, based in San Francisco, expanded their reach as they could now control distribution across California and Mexico. At the same time, Peter's connections had grown to include imports from Australia and New Zealand. On top of this, he and his brother had purchased refrigeration equipment to preserve their products (up to 2000lbs) as they sailed from ports beyond to Honolulu and finally San Francisco.

By 1892, Camarinos and Kidwell were the largest growers of pineapples in Hawai'i. Their court case, which had lasted for four years, ended with a judgment in favor of Camarinos. Kidwell tried to appeal several times but was unsuccessful. To recoup his judgment, Camarinos, with the help of Lycurgus, attempted to confiscate Kidwell's Manoa land. This proved futile because, in the same year, Kidwell formed his own corporation, the Hawaiian Fruit & Packing Company, Ltd., with $40,000 in capital. Kidwell became president, Lorrin A. Thurston served as vice-president, John Emmeluth as secretary, J. Gallagher as treasurer, and J. J. Lecker as auditor. All officers of Kidwell's new company were members of the Reform Party.

During the early 1890s, politics loomed largely, and was one of the significant factors in the development of Hawaii's pineapple industry. Kidwell was deeply involved in this political environment,

14

primarily through his association with business partners who were heavily invested in the Reform party. A party whose supporters were mainly of Protestant American Missionary decent. The Reform party that had forced a sitting monarch - King Kalākaua in 1887 to sign a new constitution that favored the wealthy white (mostly American) sugar plantation owners and disenfranchised the native Hawaiians to a greater extent. On the other side, Kidwell's rival Camarinos was a royalist and in full support of policies that bolstered the monarchy.

In 1891, at the beginning of Queen Lili'uokalani's rule, her focus was on diversifying the Hawaiian economy. Two things motivated her thoughts: the McKinley Tariff or Tariff Act of 1890, which was framed by then-Representative from Ohio – William McKinley. McKinley, a republican and future president of the United States, led the passage of this Act, and it had a disastrous effect on the Hawaiian economy, which at that point was highly dependent on the sugar industry. The import rates on sugar exports rose 35%, which resulted in the Hawaiian market being undersold, and there was an economic depression. The sugar growers knew that if Hawaii were to be annexed by the United States, the tariff problem would naturally disappear and, in turn, solve their problems. Queen Liliuokalani understood the end goal for the reformist which was another reason she desired a more diversified economy – to rid her Kingdom of any threat internal or otherwise that could further devastate her land and its people. Pineapples, as well as other crops, were vital in her plans to strengthen the economy and stabilize her nation.

On May 30th, 1892, at the opening of the Biennial Legislature Queen Liliuokalani announced, "...the appointment of a special commission (is needed)... with a view to enable the small land-holders; to add to the wealth and progress of the Kingdom by raising such products as the soil and climate of the country (will support)."

The commission recommended the establishment of a Bureau of Agriculture and Forestry, which was the first agency of this nature in Hawaii.

It would promote diversification of what was grown and

encourage small farms over the plantations. Before the commission had issued a report, Queen Liliuokalani decided to use her lands to support this objective. And with those lands comprising about a quarter of all the area in Hawaii, the potential to cause a significant shift in the economy and ultimately, the political environment was real. Camarinos, by this time, a powerful player in the pineapple industry, was in favor of the Queen's actions and tax breaks that would favor these budding agricultural endeavors. Surprisingly some sugar planters were also in favor of a diversification plan because of losses inflicted on their industry. But many were not on board with this proposition or the rest of Queen Liliuokalani's proposals. Leaders in this opposition included Kidwell, Dole, and Thurston, who, in August 1891, had already begun a campaign to wrest control of the Crown Lands from Liliuokalani. They had started leasing some Crown Lands for plantation purposes, feared her reforms, and ultimately wanted her gone. Thus, the overthrow of Queen Liliuokalani's rule was inevitable, and on January 17th, 1893, she was essentially out.

When this happened, Peter Camarinos, along with a group of her strongest supporters, began to devise a plan on how to reinstate her as monarch. This group included a great deal of the Greek community to which Camarinos was a member. Camarinos became a key member in a plot to take back the governance of the islands in 1895 – a campaign which was quickly crushed; Governor Dole declared martial law, and the Queen, along with 190 individuals were arrested. This included Camarinos, who, after serving a jail sentence, was exiled. With his property confiscated, he left for California and never returned. Unfortunately, he never recovered from his involvement and support for the Queen and died on December 8th of 1897, in a California Asylum for the Insane under mysterious circumstances.

However, Kidwell did not benefit from the demise of his strongest rival or the overthrow of the Hawaiian Kingdom. Initially, his business grew as he acquired more land and improved his cannery.

Canning was invented in France shortly after the French

Revolution. Napoleon offered a reward to anyone who could come up with a way to feed his large military. In 1809 Nicolas Appert was awarded the prize when he came up with the idea for preserving food, which is virtually unchanged today. This process eventually made its way to the United States in 1817 and became extraordinarily successful in Baltimore at the start of the 1850s. So much so, Baltimore became the epicenter of the cannery business in America.

Kidwell and his partners hired an expert from Baltimore to run their cannery. Baltimore had experience with canned pineapples, which had been done in the city since 1865. Their pineapple came from the Caribbean, which also had developed a lucrative industry. They hoped bringing an expert would further improve their product. Unfortunately, the expert Kidwell & Company hired knew little more than the locals. Frustrated Kidwell took over the development of the cannery business.

During this period, Governor Dole showed his support for the industry by continuing a law enacted under the Queen, which encouraged the cultivation, canning, and preserving of pineapples to diversify the economy away from sugar. This law specified for ten years beyond 1892, all tools, machinery, appliances, buildings, and all other personal property used in the cultivation, canning, or preserving of pineapples were exempt from all taxes. Furthermore, anything imported for use in the process of delivering crop to market was also duty-free for ten years. Despite all these advantages, duties on pineapple exports to America proved too much for Kidwell, and he never saw much of a profit off his crops. He retired in 1898 and moved to a street (1835 Wilder Avenue) near his original farm in Manoa.

Kidwell's previous missteps, misfortunes, and lack of business acumen prevented him from reaching a higher plateau in an industry he essentially started in Hawaii. Had he lasted a couple of years more, he would have probably became the most powerful grower in the history of pineapple. In the same year of his retirement, 1898, the Republic of Hawaii saw their dreams come true when the United States annexed the islands. Upon annexation, all exports to the U.S.

became duty-free and allowed Hawaii farmers to be on equal ground with growers on the mainland.

(Site of Kidwell first pineapple crop, Manoa Valley – Univ. of Hawaii Manoa)

(Luna on horse oversees workers – Hawaii State Archives)

Chapter 4

The Pineapple King

(Library of Congress – G. G. Bain Collection)

In the following year of 1899, as the century turned, the most influential individual in the Hawaiian pineapple story arrived. James Dole was born September 27, 1877, in Jamaica Plain, Massachusetts (now part of Boston), to a Puritan American family. With strong beliefs in Christianity and following the Scriptures, Puritans hope that by setting a good example, others will see and change their sinful ways.

If you look at the oligarchy or Big Five companies that shaped Hawaii of today, most of those roots tie directly back to the original missionaries from New England. Their influence spread initially from religion, quickly into the cultural fabric, the economy, and finally, politics.

James Dole, once dubbed the "Pineapple King," was a hardworking and innovative man. But his rise to the top would not have been possible if not for his connection to political and financial insiders of the time. Governor Stanford Dole was a very close first cousin to his father. So close, James' father, Charles Fletcher Dole, lived with the Governor when he moved to Hawaii in 1909.

Stanford Dole was born in Hawaii and was the son of American Protestant missionaries who moved to the islands from Maine. They were tasked with the running of Oahu College, now known as Punahou School. Stanford left the islands to attend Harvard but eventually returned and rose to prominence in politics and law. His leadership in the collation that overthrew the queen led to him becoming the President of the Republic of Hawaii and its first governor upon annexation by the United States.

When his young cousin, James Dole, arrived in 1899, their connection was more like an uncle to his nephew. Gov. Dole was in the midst of a crisis in the form of the bubonic plague that was devastating the island and led him to shelter young James during his arrival. Once the plague scares subsided, Gov. Dole assisted his cousin in gaining the proper connections to pursue his Hawaiian dreams. Through his cousin, James was able to obtain land in the upper Oahu valley of Wahiawa and began life as a farmer.

Land and its use in Hawaii had changed drastically since Capt. Cook first landed in 1778. The most dramatic changes occurred when the twelve missionaries' groups from New England arrived from 1820 to 1848. It is noteworthy that these twelve missions had additional individuals not directly tied with the gospels among their settlers. Teachers, physicians, farmers, and a host of other professionals were included in their numbers. As time passed, many sensing opportunities in the secular world began to move quickly away from the church and forge inroads in Hawaiian society.

Even individuals in the ministry began to switch from the church for opportunities elsewhere. Reverend William Richards, for example, came to the islands and initially set up a mission on the island of Maui. He would eventually become a trusted advisor and diplomat for the royalty of Hawaii and leave the church altogether. Kamehameha III requested his assistance in drawing up formal laws for his increasingly western-influenced government. The first land right reforms that gave individuals more substantial claims to property came under his influence in new policies prescribed in 1839, then further formalized in the 1840 Constitution of the Hawaiian Kingdom.

Another factor that cannot be dismissed as an acceleration of land-use changes was the decimation of the Hawaiian population due to diseases introduced by western people. It is estimated that in Hawaii, there were around 250,000 individuals of Hawaiian descent when Cook first arrived. Forty years later, less than 150,000 Hawaiians existed; forty years more, Hawaiian numbers hovered around 70,000. Early in the twentieth century, about 1920, there were only 24,000 pure-blooded Hawaiians in Hawaii, although marriages with other groups increased the size of the part-Hawaiian population. Today the number of those with some Hawaiian blood has again approached 150,000 (which is only 17 percent of the population in the state); pure-blooded Hawaiians compose only 1 percent of the residents on the islands.

Land use before outside influence was shared based on an ancient system in which an area of land division called an ahupua'a was vital. An ahupua'a ran from the tops of mountain ranges to the sea below, similar to the division of a pie. The size of an ahupua'a was dependent on the resources contained within. Under this system, all Hawaiian land was subject to the king's discretion.

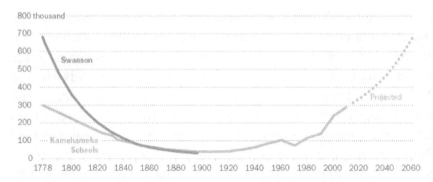

Native Hawaiian Population Makes a Comeback After Sharp Decline

Estimates of the Native Hawaiian population in Hawaii

Note: Swanson data counts only Native Hawaiian population; Kamehameha Schools includes those who are Native Hawaiian alone and in combination with other races in 2000 and after.
Sources: David Swanson, "A New Estimate of the Hawaiian Population for 1778, the Year of First European Contact";
Kamehameha Schools 2014. Ka Huaka'i: 2014 Native Hawaiian Educational Assessment. Honolulu: Kamehameha Publishing

PEW RESEARCH CENTER

An ahupua'a was held in trust by a local chief based on rank. This chief was responsible for the use of the land and how smaller units were assigned to families. This system worked best when population numbers were thriving and thus could sustain the resources within an area. The people were dependent on the land, and its resources and a sense of communal responsibility maintained its vitality. The combination of declines in Hawaiian populations and western values based on individual rights effectively weakened the control natives had on their lands.

Land from which James Dole would initially build his fortune, came about due to the Land Act of 1895. This Act gave the government more power to convert government and former crown lands into settlements where those who resided on the property could effectively lay sole claim to it. The Wahiawa Tract came from government land put up in a lease to purchase scheme by the Republic of Hawaii. With the idea of diversification of agricultural output, purchases of this property opened to a select group of individuals.

Byron O. Clarke, the Secretary and Commissioner of the Hawaii Bureau of Agriculture secured a good portion of it for himself and immigrants from California. He had emigrated from California in 1897 and was appointed Commissioner of Agriculture the following year. Before his appointment, he had been a farmer without success in the islands and had no administrative experience.

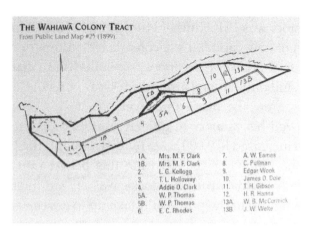

THE WAHIAWĀ COLONY TRACT
From Public Land Map #25 (1899)

1A.	Mrs. M. F. Clark	7.	A. W. Eames
1B.	Mrs. M. F. Clark	8.	C. Pullman
2.	L. G. Kellogg	9.	Edgar Wook
3.	T. L. Holloway	10.	James O. Dole
4.	Addie O. Clark	11.	T. H. Gibson
5A.	W. P. Thomas	12.	H. R. Hanna
5B.	W. P. Thomas	13A.	W. B. McCormick
6.	E. C. Rhodes	13B.	J. W. Welte

The Wahiawa Colony Tract offered up land to 16 homesteader families on lots in size from 50 to 250 acres after the grazing leases for the property ran out. Three of the homesteaders occupying four of the most significant allotments were none other than Clark's wife, brother-in-law, and child. Californians got a bulk of the other minus two lots, one of which - a lot of around 60 acres was saved for Dole. Dole's lot cost him approximately $4,000, which is equivalent to about $121,000 today. Dole's direct ties to Hawaii's inner circle would prove to be more beneficial to his fortunes than even Commissioner Clarke's were for the securement of his land.

The Wahiawa Tract quickly moved to focus on a specific crop. A consortium was formed, and the cultivation of choice became pineapple. Commissioner Clarke's left his office in 1900, the pineapple business by 1906, and the islands by the 1930s.

The initial slips used to start these farmers' endeavors were taken from the abandoned (Ewa) farm of Kidwell. Clarke knew where Kidwell had dumped his plantings, fished them out of a ditch, and planted them on his land. Many collectives formed between these homesteaders, but the most successful was the Hawaiian Pineapple Company, established in 1901, with Dole as the leader.

Within two years from their start, James Dole had convinced local and mainland businesspeople to invest in the venture. One of these investors was J.H. Hunt of Hunt Foods of San Francisco. With an infusion of new capital, Dole constructed a cannery on land next to his fields. Initially, his cannery operated with hand-operated machinery and only canned around 1,900 cases. As his knowledge of the process grew, he made improvements to his production line which allowed his cannery to quickly multiply its output. By 1904 production increased to 9,000 cases followed by another gigantic leap to 25,000 the following year. During this period transporting the product from Wahiawa to the docks was an arduous journey. A journey from farm to the port could take up to a week and involved a horse-drawn wagon trudging across rough, unpaved, and often muddy roads. Dole realized the inefficiency and loss this had on the collective and sought assistance to get his product to market.

(Dole far right – Hawaii State Archives)

Chapter 5

Relationships

(W. Dillingham – 1921, Men of Hawaii)

Walter F. Dillingham was born in 1875 to Benjamin Franklin D. Dillingham, a Massachusetts-born seaman who came to the islands in 1865. He started from humble beginnings as a clerk in a hardware store, which he eventually bought, and went on to amass an impressive number of businesses in Hawaii. One of his most notable was the Oahu Railway and Land Company. Benjamin's initial vision was to connect the Ewa plains where sugarcane production had begun to Honolulu's ports. His railway not only accomplished this by 1889 but eventually extended to the far reaches of the North Shore, where he built a hotel.

James Dole became acquainted with Walter in Boston when they both attended Harvard. Walter left Harvard before graduation to return to Hawaii. Once home, Walter began working for his father; then the Dowsett Company, a property management firm. Walter Dillingham took control of his father's businesses due to his failing health in the early 1900s. Soon after, Dole came to ask if he would be willing to build a railroad line into the central valley of Oahu. Dillingham had always been a strong supporter of Dole's efforts and because of their familiarity, Walter was more than willing to invest. He had already formed a business relationship with his college friend years before when Dole leased 300 acres from him. Dillingham and Dole agreed to the expansion between Waipahu and Wahiawa, and construction began. In 1906 the 11-mile extension was complete with the line running through the Waikakalua Gulch. This gave Dole a more reliable way to bring goods to the market, and Dillingham gained more control over the transportation infrastructure and a firmer hold into the pineapple industry.

In 1907, Dillingham also gained a direct connection to the top circles of Hawaii's political structure through his brother-in-law. Dillingham's sister Mary Emma was married to Walter F. Frear, who served as Governor from 1907 till 1913. During this period, Dillingham's businesses and influence grew in direct relation to the islands, including gaining more dredging rights in Pearl Harbor and the acquisition of the Ala Moana area of Honolulu. Dole also benefited during this period; Dillingham's investments gave his plantation more land and a direct connection to his new cannery in Iwelei, near the port, which included two warehouses and an office building.

Dole's production rose to 168,000 cases, and his climb from small-time collective farmer to a true giant of the industry was complete. 1907 was a remarkable year for Dole, but panic in markets within the United States threatened the growth of all industries in the islands. This caused Dole and his counterparts to start thinking of ways to curb any potential loss by improving how their product was marketed. The canners' concern only grew when word of their dismal sales reached the islands from sales representatives.

On May 7, 1908, nine of the pineapple canners founded the Hawaiian Pineapple Growers' Association or HPGA, an organization for the promotion of their product. Dole became its first president. The new cooperative first began by evaluating where they were selling pineapple and found where they weren't - in major urban areas with populations over 100,000; their influence was relatively small. The next items the new group decided to tackle was reaching these untapped markets with potentially millions of dollars in sales. A focus was made to put their sales agents in urban areas and increase the availability of their products in urban stores. This proved difficult initially, but in less than a year, they were growing their store visibility of major markets ten-fold.

Next, this formation of canners decided to place national advertising that promoted Hawaii's product as a unified brand – a brand that outclassed all others because of where it was grown. Before this, all companies in Hawaii which went under different names (sometimes multiple in one company). The cooperative decided to promote the brand of Hawaii as a whole. No one brand or collection of brands were to be featured. The main point was this is a Hawaiian pineapple which is in a class of its own. Dole and the other Hawaiian canners decided that an expenditure of $50,000, or about three percent of the present value of their products, would be a good starting point to launch their campaign.

One canner -Will B. Thomas, justified the use of advertising by stating, "...the packers will have to do a lot of missionary work among the consumers first... Of the eighty million people in the United States, probably half of them have never tasted pineapples, and the majority of the balance have looked upon them as a luxury...(only to be indulged in on special occasions)...(Thomas 1908). Ad campaigns from this point forward promoted the various ways and benefits of pineapple – Hawaiian Pineapple. As a side promotion of the product, Hawaii itself got showcased – "Hawaii an idealist paradise of luxury and pleasure that everyone should visit."

This was perfect advertising for all involved. Just years earlier in 1901 W. C. Peacock, a wealthy saloon and landowner, built Beaux Arts Moana Hotel on Waikiki Beach. Soon after, the first true campaign to promote tourism was undertaken in San Francisco, which at the time was about a 5-days ride via steamships. The success and excitement of this endeavor pushed business and political concerns to form the first tourism bureau in 1903. From that point forward tourism would become a key and important component in the growth of the islands. It is in this climate that the pineapple industry began its growth and its advertising eventually was used to promote itself and Hawaii. Pineapple was a perfect agricultural partner to place in the quiver of incentives used to the lure individuals to Hawaii. It represented something its bigger agricultural cousin, sugar, could not – appeal. Having a long-established relationship with royalty and its exotic nature made pineapple an enticement that could lure many to the shores of the islands.

Another layer of this new strategy was a lowering of the cost of pineapple from Hawaii compared to other markets. Canners in Hawaii, many who had little to no idea of the need for time to change consumers' minds, worried initially that growth would not come without a reduction. They speculated that the cost of their product could be the primary reason for their downturn in growth. Pineapple from the islands had historically been more expensive than products from British Malayan (Singapore) and the Bahamas, their biggest rivals but many factors played into this higher price point. It was agreed the national cooperative advertising would help add value to Hawaiian pineapple but without a price reduction their industry could fail before a turnaround could be achieved.

As a result of the HPGA's approach they started to infiltrate new markets, bigger markets, and make Hawaii more synonymous with the fruit. As a result, the value and stature of the product rose. This eventually let them reflate the price to old standards as they continued to gain market share. "It cannot be denied that their small investment in untapped markets, slick Madison Avenue advertising, and reduced-price (however slight) made rich men of many who had come from more humble beginnings", Dole exclaimed.

This first round of collective success caused them to start the second wave of national marketing before finally disbanding their first collective in 1910. Even as they decided to cut ties, they realized the strength they had gained through cooperation and decided to continue some work jointly. They formed the Association of Hawaiian Pineapple Packers (AHPP) in 1912. "Its aims were to promote the common interests of its membership, encourage the scientific development of the pineapple industry, to work for an adequate labor supply, to institute improvements in canning methods, to advance high standards for the finished products, to extend the demand for canned pineapple through judicious advertising, to improve transportation facilities and to secure the enactment of laws beneficial to the industry." (*Canning Trade October 17, 1921, 12; Honolulu Star-Bulletin: Progress and Opportunity Edition October 20, 1924, 26*) The continuation of associations on some level existed until the 1970s when the Hawaiian industry as a whole became too weak to promote the fruit. Associations still exist today, in other countries, but their effects on the worldwide pineapple industry are minor compared to Hawaiian associations throughout most of the 20th century.

The industry leaders had come together many times from the very beginning to help secure and ensure the success of pineapple. Their strategic moves helped safeguard the viability and demand for pineapple. And as important as these decisions were nothing done on that front was as vital to the industry and culture at large as the people who literally worked the product. These were groups who dealt directly with the product, in the fields, on cannery floors and the loading docks. People who came from aboard and became the backbone of industry and culture in Hawaii.

(Hawaiian Pineapple Packers Assoc.)

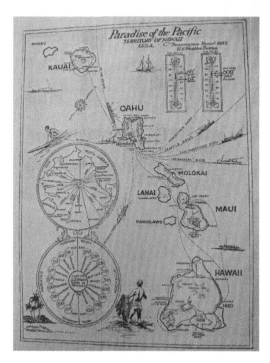

(Hawaiian Pineapple Packers Assoc.)

31

Picked Ripe Canned Right

Always put up in sanitary cans. Untouched by hand.

Hawaiian Pineapple

No other climate or soil can produce that exquisite deliciousness of flavor, that delightful tenderness, or that appetizing wholesomeness.

Hawaiian pineapples are picked ripe and canned right—the freshness of ripeness, and the flavor of Nature, going into the cans. Other pineapples are picked green—artificial ripening gives artificial flavor.

A can of Hawaiian pineapple brings to your table the ripeness, richness, and flavor of the pineapple on the field, thousands of miles away.

All dealers sell them—sliced, grated, or crushed.

Drop postal for book of Hawaiian Pineapple recipes and pictures.

Hawaiian Pineapple Growers' Association, Tribune Building, New York City

(McClure Magazine)

Chapter 6

Immigrants Welcome?

In 1853, indigenous Hawaiians made up 97% of the islands' population and were the first cultivators of pineapple in Hawaii. Hawaiians as a group by 1923 had been reduced to only 16% of the population. This decline in numbers can be attributed to many factors, including the cultural ignorance westerners showed to their way of life, political interference, and, most importantly, interaction with diseases they had no immunity to. All these hardships in quick fashion reduced their numbers and led Hawaiians to be less inclined to work on plantations. Plantation work is heavily labor-intensive, and owners needed to fill their workforce with inexpensive hands. They turned to outside sources to meet these demands. Their ideas were like their American compatriots in the south. However, with slavery prohibited, Hawaiian plantation owners sought out individuals in countries of perceived lesser development, importance, and economic stature. The countries that fit their criteria were mainly from Asia and included China, Japan, Korea, and the Philippines.

The first significant non-European wave to arrive were the Chinese. In truth, their presence in Hawai'i goes almost as far back as Captain Cook's arrival in 1778. As early as 1789, Chinese arrived aboard trading ships, and by 1794 a Chinese individual was reportedly living in the Islands. The Chinese arrival proceeded any other group used primarily as a labor force, and because of this, their work on sugar plantations far exceeds the number of Chinese who worked in the pineapple fields. The first large Chinese recruited group came under five-year contracts at $3.00 a month plus passage, food, clothing, and a house. An advance of $6 was made in China to be refunded in small installments.

In short, the plantation contract, which functioned much as it would have during feudal times, was a dismal way of life. Wages for work compared to conditions and living arrangements were substandard and not much different from the lives many were trying to escape at home. Once contracts expired, many Chinese would not renew, but instead, move to urban areas where they would compete with natives for employment. This, in turn, created tension between the Chinese and the native population. Hawaiians already suffering began to feel even more displaced by the increase in Chinese and competition brought thereon. Despite this, Chinese immigrants found better opportunities and became one of the first major contributors to the beginnings of Hawaii's middle class. They established many businesses and a healthy community. Their main area of settlement became the first Chinatown on the islands, located in central Honolulu near the ports.

Between 1876 and 1900, approximately 45,000 Chinese immigrated to Hawaii. The Chinese, regardless of short tenure on plantations, contributed significantly to their success. The Chinese offered valuable knowledge to the planters "during the early stages of the industry in Hawaii." "Planters had no knowledge of raising sugar on a commercial basis (and thus turned to the Chinese who were more versed in the production of the crop." Even with this need for expertise and labor, several issues surfaced with the Chinese worker situation." By the early 1880s, the Chinese constituted "one-fourth of the population in the islands," and by the 1884 census, in Hawaii, more than half of the male population between the ages of 15 and 50."

Despite the need for labor, "cheap labor," the importation of individuals who were not of European descent from these early stages began to worry the elite class who were rapidly westernizing and shaping the future of the islands. Yet the lack of interests from their countrymen to take up these agricultural tasks left them no choice but to find other options.

(Chinese family 1893 – Hawaii State Archives)

In the spring of 1882, the U.S. Congress passed the Chinese Exclusion Act under President Chester A. Arthur. The Act provided an absolute 10-year moratorium on the immigration of Chinese labor into America. A side effect of this Act included the restricting of Chinese immigration in the islands. To please its most important trading partner, the U.S. - Hawaii passed a law in 1883 to restrict immigration from China. Laws were quickly passed that allowed only 600 individuals within a 3-month period in for settlement. This effectively halted Chinese immigration and their involvement with Hawaiian plantations. Fifteen years later, with the annexation of Hawaii by the U.S. in 1898, the Chinese would face even more significant hurdles to their growth in Hawaii. In the U.S. Large scale, Chinese immigration would not occur again until the passage of the Immigration and Nationality Act of 1965.

The first group with a significant impact on pineapple plantations were the Japanese. When the U.S. and subsequently Hawaii passed laws to exclude the Chinese, the importation of Japanese labor had already begun in the islands. The Japanese community that came can be grouped into two distinct categories; the "Uchinanchu" or Okinawans and the "Naichi" or Mainlanders. These are terms derived from the Okinawan dialect and not words that would have been used by individuals who immigrated from the Islands of Kyushu and Honshu - considered the main islands of Japan. Okinawans spoke in a very distinct dialect because of their distance from the main islands and proximity to China. This, along with perceived differences in customs and physical appearances, created friction between the groups. In 1885 two years after the Chinese restrictions were in place, Japanese labor increased dramatically. The population grew even faster between 1898 to 1900 when around 38,000 Japanese were admitted as new arrivals. By 1907 the total population of Japanese immigrants was about 44,000, with one-fifth of them having originated from Okinawa.

At this time tensions from the increase of immigrants coming from Asia to America, in particular, California pushed the Japanese government to enter into a Gentleman's Agreement with the U.S. In this, Japan agreed not to issue passports for Japanese citizens wishing to work in the continental United States, thus effectively halting new Japanese immigration and again severely limiting immigration to Hawaii. The United States, in exchange for this halt, agreed to accept the presence of Japanese immigrants already residing in the U.S., and permit those with families the right to send for their wives, children, and parents.

The agreement was also to provide legal protection for Japanese American children who were prone to discriminatory practices, especially on the West Coast. Later in 1924 amid rising tensions in Hawaii – now a territory - and the western United States, the Federal Immigration Act was introduced. This law included a provision excluding from entry any alien who was ineligible for citizenship by virtue of race or nationality. Existing nationality laws already in place prevented people of Asian lineage from naturalizing. Because of this Act, even Asians not previously prevented from immigrating – the Japanese in particular would no longer be admitted to the United States. By this time, however, over 200,000 individuals of Japanese descent had migrated to Hawaii as plantation laborers. This Act put a complete moratorium over people coming from Japan and the rest of Asia. However, this had no lasting effects on the plantation industry, and many leaders in Hawaii praised the halts as they felt Japanese numbers were increasingly growing too large. The Philippines, now a territory of the United States, could fill the gap, and they became the next significant group to immigrate to the islands.

(Japanese servants Manoa residence – Hawaii State Archives)

The annexation of the Philippines occurred on December 10, 1898, through the Treaty of Paris – this was a godsend to the planters as it broadened their options for a viable workforce. As American subjects, Filipinos could be recruited for work on the Hawaii plantations without any immigration restrictions. Between 1906 and

1930, the HSPA (sugar industry alone) had brought in approximately 120,000 Filipinos to Hawaii. A steady increase in numbers between those years eventually made the Filipino community the most significant percentage of any workforce within the plantation system.

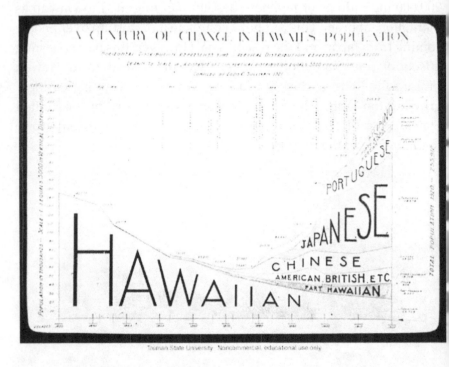

The growth of plantation-based agriculture and the dominant position those originally from western countries had over the industry shaped its development profoundly. These owners, with close ties to the U.S., developed Hawaii like a colonized country. By the end of the 19th century, the new economy and population loss had displaced and marginalized remaining Native Hawaiians; predominantly, U.S. investors had control over business and lands. Plantation managers segregated worker populations by ethnicity, much as their contemporaries did in other colonized regions of the world. The plantation economy encouraged clear stratification, with Euro-American— or haole —owners and managers on top, Portuguese field bosses, and Asian laborers. A similar hierarchy evolved in business circles, with large sugar factors, merchant houses, and banks dominating downtown Honolulu. Native Hawaiians and immigrant Asians were again regulated to populating almost the entirety of the service sector.

(Filipinos in field – Hawaii State Archives)

Under western leadership, the majority vote was suppressed through various laws, which ensured that no other group other than that of European heritage would be given a chance at leadership. To bolster these western immigration numbers and create another stratification class, more groups were recruited for immigration to the islands. These groups contributed to the cultural flavor of Hawaiian plantations even if they had little effect on the overall ethnic mix, which was occurring in Hawaii. These groups included the Portuguese, Puerto Ricans, Koreans, Russians, Spanish, Norwegians, and Germans.

The Russians, Norwegians, Spanish, and Germans had little effect on plantation life and culture, especially as concerned with pineapple. The story behind their importation, however interesting, did not effectively change ethnic ratios as hoped when these schemes were presented by leaders in the islands. The groups that would make more significant impacts on Hawaiian culture were the Portuguese, Koreans, and Puerto Ricans.

The Portuguese immigrated to Hawaii from 1878 to 1911, and during that period, around 16,000 made the trip. The Portuguese mainly came from islands off the shore of Portugal, primarily Madeira and the Azores.

This was per the suggestion of Jason Perry (Jacinto Pereira), a Portuguese settler who served as the Portuguese Consul to Hawaii. In 1876 he suggested to plantation owners that persons of Madeira and Azores might be the perfect fit for their plantations. Portuguese colonists had first settled these islands in the Middle Ages, and the climate as well as a mainstay crop on the islands, sugarcane, made them well suited for a similar life in Hawaii. Unlike the Chinese and Japanese who came primarily as single men, the Portuguese came as families. This made them more likely to plant permanent roots once they hit the shores of Hawaii. Although overall receiving more favorable treatment than the Chinese and Japanese, they still faced an uphill battle.

The elites primarily of European descent thought of the Portuguese as an inferior class regardless of their European backgrounds. But that background did ensure they were offered superior contracts to immigrant workers from Asia. Many received an acre of land, better working conditions, and job titles, often serving as luna or supervisors. Later, when the U.S. annexed Hawaii, they were also granted American citizenship. This came in handy for those who felt mistreated by the powers that be in the islands. Those who stayed had to suffer through some trauma from being treated less favorably than others with European backgrounds. However, the opportunities afforded the Portuguese once their plantation days ended were far greater than a majority of their Asian counterparts.

Puerto Ricans, on the other hand, were treated even less favorable than the Portuguese. Puerto Rican immigration began when Puerto Rico's sugar industry was devastated by two hurricanes in 1899. The devastation caused a worldwide shortage of sugar and a huge demand for the product from Hawaii. Hawaiian sugarcane plantation owners began to recruit the jobless, but experienced, laborers in Puerto Rico. Once in Hawaii, they experienced discrimination and bigotry in much the same manner as their Asian counterparts.

At the turn of the 1900s, Puerto Rico and Hawaii were unincorporated and incorporated territories of the United States respectively; however, the passage of the Jones–Shafroth Act of 1917, the same year that the United States entered World War I, granted American citizenship to the Puerto Rican resident in Puerto Rico, and excluded those who resided in Hawaii, giving them yet another disadvantage in the islands. Unfortunately, this did not preclude them from being assigned draft numbers and obligations to military duty if called upon. Where territorial status had been very favorable to the plantation owners, Puerto Ricans suffered even more injustices because of it.

Another group that ventured to Hawaii's plantations to make a go was the Koreans. The first significant wave of Korean immigration started on January 13, 1903, when a shipload of Korean immigrants arrived in Hawaii to work on pineapple and sugar plantations. By 1905, more than 7,226 Koreans had come to Hawaii.

In that number were 637 women and 465 children. They came to escape the famines and turbulent political climate of Korea. Most were from small rural villages in Korea. With Hawaii, a U.S. Territory by the time of their arrival, the Organic Acts of 1900 played an essential role in their plantation experience. The Act banned contract labor; thus, it prevented Korean laborers from being locked into long-term contracts. These contracts had slowed previous ethnic group's assimilation into other fields of work. The Koreans free from this hindrance quickly ditched plantation life to live for themselves and seek other opportunities, many of which opened businesses.

Spanish immigration to Hawaii began in 1907 when the Hawaiian government and the Hawaiian Sugar Planters' Association (HSPA) decided to supplement their ongoing importation of Portuguese workers to Hawaii with workers recruited from Spain. The importation of Spanish laborers, along with their families, continued until 1913, during which more than 9,000 Spanish immigrated to the islands primarily to work on plantations. The Spanish in earnest had been in the islands since at least 1793 when Don Francisco de Paula Marín, a Spaniard, became influential in the early Kingdom of Hawaii under Kamehameha I.

Marín introduced many agricultural firsts but is noted most for his 1813 introduction of the first cultivated pineapple crop to Hawaii. His fellow countrymen arrived around 100 years after he first stepped foot on Hawaii, and most were under the impression that life here was much better on the plantation than it actually turned out to be. For this reason and others, most of this wave of Spaniards left the islands shortly after fulfilling their contracts. Then subsequently moved on to other locations in the U.S., primarily California. By the 1930s, only 1,219 of the initial 9000 Spaniards remained, making them about .3% of the total population.

The Russians who arrived were primarily from Siberia. On October 21, 1909, 200 Siberians arrived in Honolulu Harbor. They were brought here after a strike by thousands of Japanese laborers convinced plantation owners their size and influence on the industry was growing too strong. In one last-ditch effort to decrease Asian influence and increase populations of European descent, the Hawaiian Board of Immigration began the recruitment of Russians. A report issued by the Board described local planters as "willing without reserve to employ all the Caucasian workers the government can bring to the islands, at a wage one-third larger" than what was paid, Asian laborers. A Russian named A.W. Perelstrous, a contractor for the Trans-Siberian Railroad, played an important role in this recruitment scheme.

He had met a Hawaiian plantation manager named James Low in Vladivostok, Russia. Low encourage him to take a vacation to Hawaii. On his vacation, he had the opportunity to meet with Governor Walter Frear, the brother in law of Walter Dillingham, Oahu Railways' President and an individual whose investment in the plantation system was already large and growing. They agreed on an effort to recruit Siberians in the hope they would provide a counterbalance to the powerful unions of Asian labor. This was similar in thought to earlier attempts made with the Portuguese and Spanish.

The anti-Asian sentiment was ever increasing as unions continued to make more robust demands for equal treatment, wages, and working conditions. To recruit his countrymen, Perelstrous presented false claims of prosperity to be had in Hawaii. Unfortunately for Perelstrous, his recruitment was over as quickly as it started. When he returned to Hawaii with a third wave of immigrants from Siberia, the only greeting he received upon debarking came from the previous two waves of disgruntled Russians.

The Russians he recruited were experiencing a different paradise than had been promised. On April 1, 1910, this disgruntled group went on strike and made demands like their Asian counterparts. This pushed government officials to make a last ditched effort to appease them. Meeting at 'Iolani Palace, they were presented with the best terms the planters were willing to offer. The terms were rejected, and a riot ensued as the group attacked Perelstrous shouting, "We would rather starve and die," than work the fields. Reaching an impasse, the Russians were essentially left to fend for themselves. Of the roughly 1,500 who had made the venture, few decided to tough it out in Hawaii. Most ended up back in Russia or on the West Coast of the U.S., primarily in California. Those who did stay initially set up camp in the red-light district of Iwilei, an area near the docks. They built colorful shantytowns and were reduced to taking charity and selling whatever helped in their survival. Eventually, this group assimilated into society working at the pineapple canneries, sawmills, stores. A few even returned to the plantations that had initially caused their dissatisfaction.

This experiment primarily done to effect change on the racial demographic of Hawaii ended up costing the government $143, 581, or about $3.7 million dollars today. Democratic rule had no place in plantation-era Hawaii. An oligarchy ruled the politics and economy across the archipelago. Plantation immigrants struggled to carve out a life for themselves in a land controlled almost exclusively by large commercial interests.

The early days of pineapple required hands-on labor – literally. If a field needed clearing, workers used mule teams to remove brush, trees, and stones. Once the debris was removed, mules would draw plows through the fertile volcanic soil in preparation for planting the crop. Then slips were put into the ground by hand. The process got no less labor-intensive at harvest. Workers earned every penny they got from their employers.

The hierarchy on the plantation was very delineated by race that also determined class. White or haole was exclusively put in the managerial or professional positions. It did not matter what education or experience one may have; your race would determine your potential for accomplishing a job. After 1910 the overwhelming number of workers on a plantation, sugar, or pineapple were as follows: Portuguese, Japanese, and Filipino. This is also the order of how these groups were ranked on the plantation. Filipinos were overwhelmingly put into the unskilled labor positions. Portuguese almost exclusively received supervisory and skilled jobs. Japanese workers would fall somewhere in between filling the gaps on both sides and the middle semi-skilled occupations. If you compare numbers of workers with the percentage of jobs, especially in the early 1900s, this bears out.

Average Occupational Daily Wage with Differences Based on Race, 1910

	Filipino	Japanese	"American"/white
Cane cutters	$0.69	$0.99	
Carpenters		$1.28	$4.36
Overseers		$1.25	$3.01

Source (Takaki 1983: 77)

These stratifications of the workforce were, of course, intentional. The primary reason being for the plantation (Euro) class could maintain a hierarchal advantage and assure they and their descendants would have control and favor over the economy for decades to come. It also kept advancement to a minimum by presenting a ceiling to how far you could be promoted. This, in turn, suppressed an increase in wages because a promotion was almost an impossibility. The system also worked well, keeping these groups from joining each other to fight for better conditions. Salaries were dependent on your racial background regardless of occupation.

If an ethnic group decided to go on strike in pre-WWII Hawaii, the opposing group would receive more incentives to break the strike, thus sowing seeds of jealousy and distrust that, in turn, hurt everyone's chances of advancement. This was a struggle primarily between the Filipino and Japanese communities. The Portuguese were involved in their own struggle, a struggle to be

45

considered white. As in the continental U.S., the delineation of white and others was quite different from interpretations today. It should be noted that categories like "Asian-American" did not exist and the race of Asians and Europeans was determined more by ethnicity. Portuguese were determined to be a race separate from Northern Europeans, making them closer in kin but not worthy of all the advantages of being part of the Caucasian race.

An excellent example of this was a letter written by a third-generation Portuguese woman, "a university graduate and social worker":

It is a shame that just because our ancestors came here as laborers, with low economic status, that their children, for generations, have been made to feel keenly inferior through prejudicial practices in the Islands.

The year and a half I spent in California proved to me that prejudice against the Portuguese is very slight there as compared with here. Neither there, nor in any other states, do prejudicial "Other Caucasians" and "haole" classifications exist. There we are "Caucasian," and as such, are accepted in accordance with individual merits.

In plantation Hawaii, everyone had their limits if you were not at the top of the pyramid. The workday for all not in the ruling class was long, and both on and off the job, workers' lives were strictly controlled by the plantation. Each planter hired a private army comprised of individuals mostly of European ancestry who oversaw a group of individuals primarily of Asian origin.

These overseers enforced company rules by any means necessary. Severe fines and harsh punishments were not out of the ordinary. Whippings were not uncommon, and these punishments could be imposed for several offenses. Talking, smoking, or pausing in the field to stretch were valid reasons to receive the wrath of a luna, the Hawaiian word that translates literally to high or above. On the plantation, it meant boss or supervisor who was typically on a horse to survey the fields high above the growing pineapple or cane.

An Okinawan immigrant recalled the reaction some had to the possibility of being whipped:

Because of the perpetual fear of this unbearable whipping, some workers committed suicide by hanging or jumping in front of the on-coming train. Fortunately, we Okinawans had been trained through ages to endure hardships caused by terrible typhoons. So no one among us committed suicide. . . .(However) there was no one who wasn't whipped." - Kinji Chinzen

The thought of an individual receiving the atrocity of being beaten for not performing tasks that inevitably would be difficult for any individual brought many to a breaking point. Punishments happened daily, and lack of workers' rights left most unrecorded along with acts of resistance. As workers were technically not enslaved, many resorted to violence as a way of protest. Workers often attempted to protect themselves against the violence doled out by lunas. These acts of retaliation often brought on even harsher penalties for the workers involved. Lunas acting on behalf of the plantation owners imposed the plantation's will, leaving workers with fundamentally no control over their lives and bodies.

Chapter 7

Life on the Farm

(Workers in field, 1910 – Hawaii State Archives)

Until 1900, plantation workers were legally bound to 3 to 5-year contracts, and "deserters" could be jailed. Called Ha'alele Hana, or desertion from service, was expected as many workers found the work and living conditions intolerable. In 1892, authorities arrested 5,706 individuals for deserting their contract services on the plantations. Most of these arrests resulted in convictions. The chances of you being found not guilty were around three percent. The sentence for those convicted was usually a forced return to the plantation. Planters did of course try to prevent these escapes before it became a criminal matter. They formed surveillance networks or an informal system of mutual assistance to find and capture deserters. Others offered rewards for the capture of runaways. These "incentives" gave individuals more motivation to identify and report suspicious individuals, who were thought to be escaped "laborers" to the authorities. A vast majority of laborers had worked on farms before they arrived in Hawaii. So, the relentless toil and impersonal scale of industrial agriculture were shocking and for many unbearable. For the many who stayed, thousands fled to the mainland or their mother countries long before their contracts were up.

For those who weathered the storm, a sense of union developed as the realization that the plight of many carries a resonance stronger than the despair of one. Plantation workers began grouping together as early as 1851 to fight the harsh realities of their condition. None of these protests produced significant results until 1909. In that year, about 5,000 Japanese workers, or about 70 percent of Hawaii's plantation workers, went on strike. These were primarily sugar plantation workers, but their efforts brought change across the industry. The strike lasted four months, and police harassed and arrested strikers en masse. Many were forcibly removed from their company-provided housing, receiving twenty-four-hour eviction notices. This, in turn, forced officials in Honolulu to scramble in search of shelter for thousands of displaced individuals. Yasutaro Soga, the editor of the Nippu Jiji, wrote, "The city of Honolulu was just like a battlefield, with everything in extreme confusion." The displacement and dwindling supplies eventually drove some workers back to the fields. Then on August 5, 1909, organizers officially ended the strike. However, workers could not claim total victory until later in the year when the minimum wage was raised to twenty-two dollars a month or $620 in today's money. Although paltry wages, it was what they demanded and improved the quality of the collective. The strike was also a motivating factor, as mentioned in recruitment efforts by Hawaii's elite for people of non-Asian descent.

Over the years, even with these gradual improvements, plantation life had remained rigidly segregated by nationality -

Japanese, Chinese, and Filipino laborers tending to work and play within their own communities. These distinctions could even be condensed down beyond ethnicity to a regional level. An example of this was with the Okinawan community, who saw themselves as distinctly different from mainland Japanese, with the opposite also being true.

Regardless of this segmentation of ethnicities, you could be rest assured that every worker, regardless of background, had their life's existence strongly tied to the plantation. A contemporary observer described vividly a plantation payday, which took place once a month: " - Outside of the plantation office where the laborers received their wages, stretches a long line of vehicles, ancient and new, large and small, ranging from a rickety fish wagon to the ultra-smart coupe of an auto salesman. Each is waiting with a common purpose: to get a payment on the laborer's bill. The laborers fall in line along the walk leading to the paymaster's office window. Plantation police keep order in the line. Two stand by the window and check the bangos - a bango was a copper plate with the worker's identification number engraved on it. Workers used their bango to make purchases at the plantation store on credit and as a timeclock during work hours. It was his pass, and he is fined a dollar if he loses it. The bango must be checked to be sure each man gets his own pay envelope. The policeman hands the bango to the paymaster who returns it to the laborer with the pay envelope containing his monthly earnings after deductions for plantation store bills. Sometimes it is only a receipt that greets the eyes of the eager employee. His money has been entirely consumed in bills. Sometimes there a balance of from S2.00 to S10.00 or $15.00. Whatever may be left in the pay envelope is not infrequently consumed by the waiting line of creditors." - Roman R. Cariaga

The company store was another gift and burden for workers on plantations. Because of the distance to town and lack of alternatives, workers were dependent on the plantation store for many essential supplies and goods. A worker would be wise to keep

50

careful track of their spending habits. Those who did not could easily fall into debt as the company store was more than happy to issue credit. And why not - the store knew where to collect on its debt - the other side of its own accounting department – the one that gave payments to the workers. For this reason, falling in debt could be very detrimental to workers. A worker in debt owes time to the plantation – time spent on the plantation was something many were dying to escape: a worker's burden but plantation owner's boon.

(Plantation home, 1900s – Hawaii State Archives)

On the plantation, one could say you lived a very insular life. All your peers lived in company housing, much of which was meager and unsanitary like your own. If you were a Luna, your accommodations were considerably better, but a majority of workers who devoted ten to twelve hours of work, returned exhausted to dismal, termite-ridden bunkhouses. Conditions varied from plantation to plantation, but, typically, workers huddled together in barracks that accommodated anywhere from six to forty men — their bed - roughly, one-by-twelve wooden planks. If you were married, you fared a little better as you were given a small furnished room to accommodate your family – regardless of size.

Privacy was a luxury enjoyed by few, and workers tended to group according to their racial and ethnic identity, to past the few idle hours that emerged. Japanese workers enjoyed community baths and some traditions from their homeland. Buddhist temples sprung up on every plantation, and many had their own resident Buddhist priest. The midsummer holiday of Obon, the festival of the souls, was celebrated throughout the plantation system, and all work stopped on November 3 in celebration of the then Emperor of Japan's birthday - Emperor Meiji.

Filipinos on plantations spent their off-hours in various ways. They enjoyed playing baseball and other sports, but gambling was the most popular, with cockfights drawing the largest crowds. Cards games were popular with all groups - Sakura, which originated in Japan, was probably the most played. Taxi-dance halls were also popular. "(They) crowded the taxi-dance halls, craving the company of women... Filipino string bands, traveling from plantation to plantation, played music at dances... Filipino men eagerly purchased tickets that offered them momentary joy - three minutes to hold, touch, and dance with a woman," – Ronald Takaki The sad reality of their lives is that many did not have their wives, girlfriends, or even sufficient women to spend time with once work ended. For a time, Filipino women were so rare on the islands that men were willing to pay up to $50 for three minutes with a woman from back home.

For these men of all ethnicities, life could seem empty because of the loneliness. Those who needed comfort beyond their mental capacities could find the same vices you would expect anywhere else in the world - alcohol, drugs, gambling, and of course, prostitution. And where there is a need, entrepreneurs always find opportunities. As an example, among the 3,726 Japanese women who arrived in Hawai'i by 1900, there were likely some prostitutes. Men in Hawaii and women from Japan recognized the potential that existed in this gender gap, and a market opened. Some were legitimately trying to find substantial connections, and others just looking for comfort, found links through brokers capitalizing on this imbalance. The reality was money earned by these mostly young men barely sustained their subsistence. Regardless of this, the need for companionship pushed many to save, spend, or borrow for the opportunity to be in the arms of a woman.

For women who made it to the islands, this could be a profitable or unhappy situation. But the first hurdle for women of non-European persuasion was gaining entry into the islands. The difficulty of unmarried women to migrate to Hawai'i brought into being a new scheme for getting visas – the picture bride. During this period, picture brides were allowed as a way of "summoning families" or yobiyosei jidai and securing passage to Hawaii. These women were entered into their future husband's family registry in Japan, and upon arriving in Hawai'i, both knowingly and unwittingly, many became prostitutes rather than wives.

Pimps and madams with promises of a brighter future, either through legitimate marriages or economic opportunity, lured these gullible young women from their families and hometowns. Many who arrived were forced into this sex trade and shamed into not trying to return home with the threat of telling their family and community about their island lifestyle. A report written by the

Committee on Social Evil in May 1914 reported that some prostitutes were "brought into the Territory as picture brides, as men who desire to exploit them for their own gain." These types of acts were not confined to any one ethnic group as schemes and ideas to exploit the lack of women were prevalent.

(Picture bride (unknown) with young family – Hawaii State Archives)

(Picture bride (unknown) – Harvard University)

Another pastime all ethnic groups on the plantation enjoyed was "talking story" to pass the hours. At the boarding houses, community centers, and stores on the plantation, talking story was something everyone enjoyed. Even though individuals tended to stay in their ethnic enclaves, this way of social interaction proved to be a great way to know one another. Having to communicate, both for entertainment and mostly work, essential phrases and words that could be understood by all regardless of background emerged. From this Hawaiian Pidgin, developed – a marrying of English with mother tongues from around the world – a mix of Portuguese, Hawaiian, Cantonese, Ilocano, Tagalog, Japanese, Korean, and Scottish were among the languages or dialects that melded to help plantation workers communicate.

(Plantation life, Ewa plains – Hawaii State Archives)

Chapter 8

Pineapple Dreams

You have heard of

Hawaiian "Picked Ripe" Pineapples

But have you tasted this most delicious fruit?

It brings to your table the richest, tenderest, and most delicious pineapple in the world. The conditions that make this possible are:

The finest variety of pineapple produced, highest flavor and tenderness.

Grown in a scientific manner under climatic conditions which in Hawaii are just suited to produce pineapple perfection—rich and luscious.

Ripened on the plant, and no pineapple can be perfect that is picked until the ripening process has converted the indigestible starch of the green fruit into the wholesome and delicious sugar of the naturally ripened pineapple.

Picked at the right moment and immediately canned by the most modern mechanical process, hermetically sealed in sanitary cans, thus preventing contamination by acid or solder, sterilized by live steam. All the fragrance and sweetness of the best pineapple on earth sealed up in a can, ready for your table, at a price no higher than that of canned pears or peaches.

You can get Hawaiian Pineapple at your grocers. Be sure he doesn't give you any other pineapple, because all other pineapple is no more like Hawaiian Pineapple than a raw turnip is like a Baldwin apple.

Drop postal for booklet of recipes and pictures.

"It's so different."

Drop postal for booklet of recipes and pictures.

Hawaiian Pineapple Growers' Association, Tribune Building, New York City.

The combination of pineapple producers and their workers had made the industry a success. People on the mainland began to recognize Hawaii and the pineapple. Since Hawaii was out of reach for most Americans, many decided - why not enjoy a little taste of heaven - from a can. Hawaii's pineapple campaign was benefiting the brand and many other sectors of the Hawaiian economy. And the connections between Hawaii and the mainland became more robust, the brand value of Hawaii increased across the board. Jamaica had rum, Tahiti - Gaugin but Hawaii had Pineapple, and pineapple was poised to make quite an impact on the American palate.

The pineapple industry sold a dream, and soon grocery stores in major cities were selling out of that dream. Sales in Chicago, San Francisco, and New York rose significantly. Orders poured in, and within less than two years, they were depleting their warehouse supplies. By 1915, pineapple became the second leading industry in revenues behind sugar for Hawaii.

From that point on, the sector witnessed exponential growth most years until the 1990s. The idea to form a pineapple cooperative for the study, business, and especially advertising of pineapple helped add intrinsic value to Hawaiian canned pineapple. This helped in retailing the product at a premium price. Eat Hawaiian pineapple because it's the best! Even when canneries in Taiwan came to match the Hawaiian product's quality in the 1930s, the Hawaiian product still retailed at a higher price because the brand had been established as the best of the best. It's all about the branding!

As the branding and revenue grew, so did the industry's influence over Hawaii. In 1923, James Dole used the wealth and power of his Hawaiian Pineapple Company to purchase an entire island – Lanai - the sixth largest in the state. Before his purchase, the island had been occupied since the 15th century by small groups of inhabitants. In 1854 a group of Mormons was granted a lease of an ahupua'a – which is a Hawaiian way of dividing land from the mountain tops to the sea. The land named Pālāwai was settled by Hawaiians converted to the Mormon religion. The initial leaders left, but in 1862 Walter M. Gibson took over leadership of the group. A year later, Gibson bought the land for $3000 with money from the church but put the title in his name. When the Mormons found out they excommunicated Gibson; he decided to keep the land. By the 1870s, Gibson not only owned his original Ahupua'a but acquired most of the rest of Lanai land for ranching. He was able to do so by winning the favor of King Kalakaua, who gave his approval and political influence on his purchases. After the 1887 Bayonet Constitution, where King Kalakaua was forced to relinquish much of his authority, and his ardent supporters were pressed into lesser positions. Most of the influential class looked at Gibson as a traitor to his kind and wished him locked up or killed.

Gibson decided to flee. He left the islands never to return. His departure left the majority of Lanai in the control of his daughter, Talula Lucy Hayselden, and his son-in-law. They formed Maunalei Sugar Company in 1899, but in less than two years, the company was virtually bankrupt. During this short period of operation, nearly 800 laborers, mostly from Japan, had been contracted for the plantations. Once the plantation system failed, some of these workers moved on to other islands, stayed, or returned to Japan. Between 1902 and 1907, Charles Gay purchased large parts of Lanai. The population at that time was around 619. Gay acquired more of Lanai until he owned everything minus 100 acres; however, due to financial difficulties, this was short-lived. He was forced to transfer most of the land to W. G. Irwin, who at one time was a member of King Kalakaua's Privy Council. This left Gay with around 600 acres, and in 1921 he attempted to start a pineapple plantation, but it failed. The next year in 1922, Gay's portion, along with what was now owned by the Lanai Company, was bought by James Dole's Hawaiian Pineapple Company for 1.1 million dollars, the equivalent of 17 million dollars today.

When the Hawaiian Pineapple Company took over Lanai, it became the center of Hawaii's pineapple industry and, by default, the "Pineapple Capital of the World." This was a fulfillment of sorts for James Dole, who had come to Hawaii with a dream and used his connections and pineapples to achieve heights he probably didn't even imagine. In 1923 development of the pineapple plantation begins on a massive scale. Livestock on Lanai that had grown out of control was reduced, especially cattle. A new water system was started along with the dredging of Kaumalapau Harbor.

Lana'i City was planned and constructed along with road building. Lanai was to be no longer a sleepy little outpost trying to find an identity. Land plowed and tilled was prepared for king pineapple. The population of Lana'i in 1925 was almost no existent just ninety-nine people of mostly Hawaiian descent. The following year Hawaiian Pineapple would see its first harvest, and from that point, forward pineapple and the population of Lanai would steadily increase.

(Aerial view Lanai, 1920s – Hawaii State Archives)

Chapter 9
Goliath's Fall

Unfortunately, this high point in the industry was also the beginning of the demise of James Dole, the pineapple king. To purchase Lanai, Dole relinquished a one-third interest of his company to the Waialua Agricultural Company – a sugar producer. This was a company he had been in business with for some time. He leased land for pineapple they could not use for sugar. Waialua was, for extensive purposes, part of Castle & Cooke, who owned 20 percent of the business. Castle & Cooke, part of Hawaii's "Big Five" – a group of companies that virtually controlled the islands - had been in recent disputes with Dole over shipping contracts.

At this point, Dole felt keeping all business within this small, powerful group hurt his bottom line, but perhaps he forgot the benefits he had reaped from similar relationships in the past. As Dole was expanding his business, he started borrowing heavily - the economy was booming, and so was business – so no problem. For seven years after Lanai came online, his company continued having fabulous success, including during the beginning of the Great Depression. Dole, believing the company would be unaffected, decided to expand plant operations, which cost 5 million dollars on top of a 3.5 million he already owed to banks. When his 1931 earnings were made public, his company showed losses although still profitable. Hawaiian pineapple sold at a premium, but people could barely afford the standard fare.

On top of that, the pineapple was still thought of as an exquisite luxury, not necessarily the fruit you think of when going through hard times. As a result, his warehouses started to fill up as demand slowed. Dole lowered prices, but inventory continued to pile up, and creditors began to get anxious.

This pressure was increased due to his unwillingness to continue business as usual with the "Big Five." And this led to a major miscalculation on his part when he declined to use the primary transporter of goods from Hawaii to the mainland - Matson Navigation Co., which was partially owned by Alexander & Baldwin, Inc. – another "Big Five" company. Instead, early in 1931, he signed a three-year contract with the Isthmian Line out of New York. Henceforth, Dole became *persona non grata* in Hawaiian business and political circles. When he asked for an extension of credit, his request fell on deaf ears. This prompted him to call on banks in San Francisco – an unfortunate choice, as this was the home of Matson Navigation. Not surprisingly, his pleas in the city by the bay also went unheard. With nowhere else to turn, Hawaiian creditors put his company in the bullseye. Their focus perked the interest of companies outside of Hawaii as a takeover target and potential entry into the Hawaiian market. Castle & Cooke, who enjoyed the strength and influence of the "Big Five" companies, did not want outsiders influencing business as usual in the islands. They immediately decided to step in and take control of the leading company in Hawaii's second-largest industry. They forced their stake in the company and kicked Dole out of his leadership role.

In 1932, Castle & Cooke assumed a 21 percent stake in the Hawaiian Pineapple Company, and with Waialua's now 37 percent, they effectively had control. Dole for a time, remained on as chairman, but his leadership was only symbolic. Dole was sent on a "well-earned rest," from which he was never recalled. When he tried returning in 1933, he found his office moved to a storeroom, and Atherton Richards, from Castle & Cooke, was now leading his company. Dole stayed on as the "face" of the company for years; and received $30,000 annually for his service. This ended in 1948, when his services were deemed unnecessary.

Within four years of Castle & Cooke's takeover of the Hawaiian Pineapple Company, it returned to profitability and washed away all its debt. Joseph Atherton Richards, who was at the helm of the company, was the son of Theodore Richards and Mary

Cushing Atherton. Joseph's maternal great grandparents were part of the initial missionaries, who came to the islands - Amos Starr Cooke and Juliette Montague. Amos Starr Cooke, along with Samuel Northrup Castle, founded Castle & Cooke.

Richards, during his time as chair, foresaw the potential loss of the U.S. market to foreign competition. These first steps into foreign markets were brought about by a company that had entered Hawaii in 1917, Calpak, or California Packing Corporation, now known as Del Monte. Calpak was looking to start a farm overseas, to reduce labor costs. Why import labor when you can go to them? In 1941, Richards pushed for legislation that would ban the export of pineapple planting material, that could be used to start plantations in the Philippines or South America. His bill passed the legislature but was killed by then-Governor Poindexter with a veto. Soon after this, World War II started, and the need to worry about the export of production abroad was quelled. Richards would leave Hawaiian Pineapple later that year, primarily due to disagreements with the board, on the general direction the company should take. He moved on from the company but continued to chair or sit on the boards of many other Hawaiian companies.

Despite these first moves abroad, Hawaiian Pineapple and the rest of the industry continued to have a hold on the industry for decades to come. Some key factors worked in their favor and helped them remain healthy. First, Lanai - Think of it - an entire island dedicated to the primary production of one crop. It is not often one company can dictate virtually everything inside and out of its normal purview of control. Another significant advantage was an industry-leading invention, the Ginaca machine, for cutting pineapples.

1,039,926.

Patented Oct. 1, 1912.
4 SHEETS—SHEET 1.

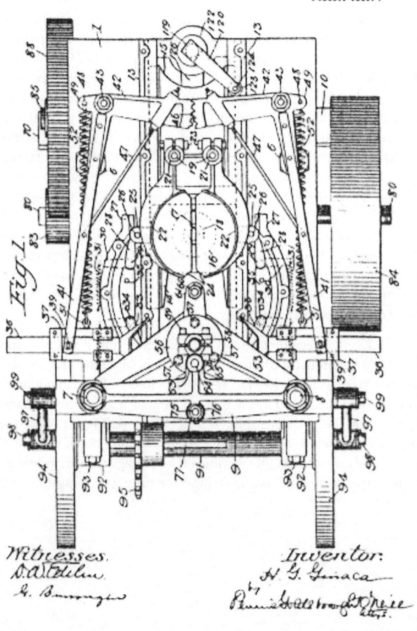

Fig. 1.

Witnesses.
D. A. Teller.
G. Banninger.

Inventor:
H. G. Ginaca

64

(Henry G. Ginaca – Dole Company)

In 1911 James Dole hired Henry G. Ginaca to design a machine to automate the process of processing pineapple. As fruit dropped through the Ginaca machine, a cylinder was cut to the proper diameter, trimmed on top and bottom, then cored. This machine more than tripled production, which quickly pushed the industry to a higher trajectory. Ginaca designed the device during his first year at Hapco and continued to improve on his design until 1914. Deciding to move on to other projects he resigned from the company. He returned to the mainland with his brothers and tried his hand at mining. Unfortunately, Henry died only seven years after his invention, an invention for which he received no patent rights and only 50 percent of profits from sales - to outside companies. Sales that never amounted to much because of fears mass dissemination of the machine could threaten the dominance of Hapco. This was probably a legitimate concern because of its innovative design. The Ginaca's machine was so successful it won a gold medal at the Panama-Pacific Exposition in San Francisco in 1915. Even today, although updated, the Ginaca machine is still the production standard for pineapple around the world.

(Ginaca machine, 1920s – Hawaii State Archives)

Another great asset to Hawaiian pineapple was the cooperative that was formed to market the fruit. In time, a research arm was added to maintain the quality, and standard people had grown to expect. The AHPC or Association of Hawaiian Pineapple Companies, was superseded in 1933 by the Pineapple Producers Cooperative Association or the PPCA. The PPCA was replaced by the Pineapple Growers Association of Hawaii in 1944, and that organization survived until early in the 21st century. The Pineapple Research Institute of Hawaii was a department of the PPCA until 1944, when it was established as a separate industry-funded non-profit research institute to distance the PPCA from thoughts of market collusion. Legal advice obtained in the late 1930s suggested the cartel was illegal. At that time, it had complete control over price, supply, and marketing.

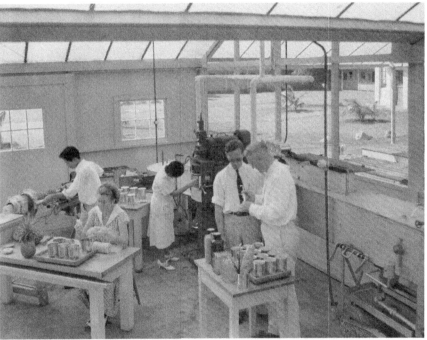

(Pineapple Research, 1934 – University of Hawaii)

A final key factor that played into the longevity of the industry was the introduction of pineapple juice on the national scale. Research and production of juice started in the early 1930s on a small scale. Once the sector recovered, those in charge at Hawaiian Pineapple decided to introduce juice on a larger scale. James Dole had played a prominent role in the development of juice but never got the opportunity to expand its production. When it finally received a promotion and launched, it became a huge success. From 6,000 cases in 1933 to a whopping 700,000 the following year. By 1936 that number had grown to 7.5 million cases. The production of juice had another benefit to growers as an outlet for the overproduction of the fruit. This growth and strength in the market kept the industry robust well into the 1960s.

During the 60s and until the 2000s, the gradual decline of the industry started. Shipments of fresh pineapple dropped off after 1996 when exports from South America produced nearly the same product. These pineapples were grown by the same companies that dominated the Hawaiian market, but with cheaper labor and shipping costs. Hawaiian companies squeezed Hawaii out of the market by competing against themselves. Finally, in 2007, Maui Land & Pineapple Co., who ran the last existing cannery, closed its production, and effectively ended the era of pineapple's dominance in the islands.

(Pineapple Washing Machine – Hawaii State Archives)

Aftermath

The circumstances that brought about the fall of the Hawaii industry are no different from those that helped its rise to glory. Globalization allowed companies to move to new locations with cheap labor and favorable laws. The only difference now is the ease with which this process can happen. Today, pineapples are grown around the world – Costa Rica, Brazil, Philippines, China, Ghana, and Nigeria are among the leaders in the industry. Hawaii's production is so minor that it accounts for less than one percent of the world's total supply. Still, the symbolic iconography that bonds the fruit to the islands exists.

The leading industries in the state today are overwhelmingly tourism and defense. Agriculture is also ranked high, third, or fourth most years, but a lot of this production is used to fuel the local market. The pineapple production is primarily for tourism with Dole Plantation ranked among the leading tourist attractions on the island of Oahu. The fruit still helps in the selling of Hawaii.

Pineapple - An industry that dominated the U.S., first with fresh product, then cans, and finally, juice reinvented itself multiple times to maintain and expand its hold on the industry. First, in the U.S. and eventually worldwide. For over 100 years, the center of pineapple production was Hawaii. And its influence on the culture, politics, and economics of the islands are still apparent.

If you look around, beyond the last fields remaining, you will see all that pineapple has done for Hawaii. It's in the bars, the lobbies, the art, and the culture. Most importantly, it's in the people whose parents and grandparents worked the plantations and now call Hawaii - their home.

Additional Photos

(Hawaiian Pineapple Company Brochure, 1920s – University of Hawaii)

(Pineapple Shipping Yard, 1920s – Hawaii State Archives)

(Barges on (Lanai, 1920s – Hawaii State Archives)

(Pineapple Field Windward Oahu, 1920s – Hawaii State Archives)

71

(Women on canning line – Hawaii State Archives)

(Ginaca machines on cannery floor – Hawaii State Archives)

(Luna and workers in the field – Hawaii State Archives)

(Woman in pineapple fields – Hawaii State Archives)

(Japanese immigrants at pier, 1890s – Hawaii State Archives)

(Mulch paper machine – Hawaii State Archives)

(Workers in the field, 1930s – Hawaii State Archives)

(Loading train to pier – Hawaii State Archives)

(Ship loading for departure, 1950s – Hawaii State Achives)

Acknowledgments

"Good writing is remembering detail. Most people want to forget. Don't forget things that were painful or embarrassing or silly. Turn them into a story that tells the truth." ~ Paula Danziger

"There is no rule on how to write. Sometimes it comes easily and perfectly: sometimes it's like drilling rock and then blasting it out with charges." ~ Ernest Hemingway

The world is a better place thanks to people who encourage and support others. What makes it even better are people who share their wisdom without looking for a return. We thank everyone who has supported us with the hope we will pay it forward.

Thanks to all we have had the opportunity to engage, work alongside, and learn from. Without the experiences gained through those encounters this book would not exist. This book began as a dream and a feature-length documentary crafted together at Olelo public access television studios in Mapunapuna. We are indebted to Olelo for providing their invaluable resources, knowledgeable and supportive staff, and for providing free speech avenues to the community of Oahu. Taking an idea and turning it into something tangible is an arduous journey. The challenge and difficulty of that path make the goal that much more rewarding.

About the Authors

David Oglesby is a writer (Nana, The Happy Face Spider) / filmmaker (A Pineapple Republic, Hiro's Table [photography], Living Doll [short]) with a 15+ year background in education. He has taught in both formal (PreK – university) and informal (museum and adult education) settings. He has an MFA from Chapman University (Orange, CA) and BA from the University of West Florida (Pensacola, FL). Hobbies include travel, golf, and movies.

Joy Ogawa is a writer and Psychologist, born and raised in Hilo, HI. She worked as a Counselor in Addiction Medicine and most recently, as a Case Manager for incarcerated women transitioning back into the community. She has a Bachelors from Santa Clara University and a couple of Masters degrees in Communication and Counseling Psychology, respectively. She currently works in Corrections/Public Safety. Hobbies include needlework, jogging, and paddling for Lokahi Canoe Club.

Notes:

Chapter 1, page 5, paragraph 1 – excerpt from
The US annexation of Hawaii, 1893(2016). Retrieved from
https://libcom.org/history/annexation-hawaii-1893

Chapter 2, page 7, paragraph 1 – excerpt from
Chapters XXXVI-XLVIII. - digital.library.upenn.edu.
http://digital.library.upenn.edu/women/liliuokalani/hawaii/ha
waii-5.html

Chapter 3, page 13, paragraph 3 – excerpt from
An English Entrepreneur in the Hawaiian Islands: The Life ....
https://evols.library.manoa.hawaii.edu/bitstream/10524/512/1/J
L31133.pdf

Chapter 5, page 27, paragraph 4 – excerpt from
Thomas, W.B. 1908. Pineapple Industry. Paradise of the Pacific 21
(December): 45. Thurston

Chapter 5, page 29, paragraph 2 – excerpt from
Canning Trade October 17, 1921, 12; Honolulu Star-Bulletin:
Progress and Opportunity Edition October 20, 1924, 26

Chapter 6, page 43, paragraph 1 – excerpt from
https://www.pri.org/stories/2015-01-28/group-siberians-hawaii-
was-far-being-tropical-paradise

Chapter 6, page 45, graph – excerpt from
Takaki, Ronald. Pau Hana: Plantation Life and Labor in Hawaii
1835-1920. Honolulu: University of Hawaii Press, 1983, 77

Chapter 6, page 46, paragraph 2 – excerpt from
Estep, Gerald A. "Social Placement of the Portuguese in Hawaii as
Indicated by Factors in Assimilation," M.A. thesis, University of
Southern California, 1941, 12

Chapter 6, page 47, paragraph 2 – excerpt from
Hawaii Times, 1 January 1959

Chapter 7, page 48, paragraph 1 – excerpt from
Nakamura, Kelli. Plantations. (2020, June 19). *Densho Encyclopedia*.
Retrieved 21:57, September 19, 2020 from
https://encyclopedia.densho.org/Plantations.

Chapter 7, page 50, paragraph 2 – excerpt from
Chapter Nine Plantation Life And Work
https://scholarspace.manoa.hawaii.edu/bitstream/10125/17992/1
/alcantara_ch_9.pdf

Chapter 7, page 52, paragraph 3 – excerpt from
Takaki, Ronald. Strangers From a Different Shore. Boston : Little,
Brown, c1998, 161

Chapter 9, page 66, paragraph 2 – excerpt from
Hawaii Pineapple: The Rise and Fall of an Industry in ....
https://journals.ashs.org/hortsci/view/journals/hortsci/47/10/a
rticle-p1390.xml

References:

Pietrusewsky, M., Douglas, M., Ikehara-Quebral, R., & Goodwin, Conrad (2017, January). The search for Don Francisco de Paula Marin: Servant, friend, and advisor to King Kamehameha I, Kingdom of Hawai'i.

Lili'uokalani, Q. (1898). Hawaii's story by Hawaii's Queen. Queen Lili'uokalani Trust.

General Catalogue Of The Officers And Graduates Of Williams College, 1905 By Williams College. https://archive.org/details/bub_gb_YRJBAAAAIAAJ/page/n71/mode/2up

Hawkins, R. A. (1997). An English Entrepreneur in the Hawaiian Islands: The Life and Times of John Kidwell, 1849−1922. *The Hawaiian Journal of History, 31*, p. 127 – 142.

Stinton, E. (2019). *Remembering the Pineapples that caused an Overthrow.* https://www.khon2.com/remembering-hawaii/remembering-the-pineapples-that-caused-an-overthrow/

What Are the "Ceded Lands" of Hawaii? U.H. law Professor Jon Van Dkyke explains key issue for future of state, both for Native Hawaiians and for general population (2010). http://-https://www.civilbeat.org/2010/10/5914-what-are-the-ceded-lands-of-hawaii/

Frangos, S. (2015, August). The Brothers Camarinos: Hawaii Pineapple Entrepreneurs Pre-Statehood. *The National Herald.*

Burton, R. L. (1986). *Canneries of the Eastern Shore.* Tidewater Publishers.

Hawaii, In-Depth History(). https://www.frommers.com/destinations/hawaii/in-depth/history#:~:text=Tourism%20in%20Hawaii%20began%20in%20the%201860s.&text=A%20tourism%20promotion%20bureau%20was,from%20San%20Francisco%20to%20Honolulu.

La Croix, S. J. (2002, January). The Economic Histroy Of Hawai'i: A Short Introduction. , *Working Paper No. 02-3.*

Hviding, J. (). *The Race for the Seaming Machine.* Stavanger Museum/Norwegian Canning Museum.

Greenspan, J. (2018). *Hawaiiâ€™s Monarchy Overthrown With U.S. Support, 120 Years Ago.* https://www.history.com/news/hawaiis-monarchy-overthrown-with-u-s-support-120-years-ago

Greaney, E. (1976). Hawaii's Big Six A Cyclical Saga . *The Encyclopedia of Hawaii,* ().

(1910). *The Apothecary.* MCP Publications, Incorporated.

Bartholomew, D. P., Hawkins, R., & Lopez, J. A. *Hawaii Pineapple: The Rise and Fall of an Industry.*

Love, A. (2018). *A Brief History of Hawaiian Agriculture.* https://gingerhillfarm.com/a-brief-history-of-hawaiian-agriculture/

Thurston, L. A. (1897). *A Hand-book on the Annexation of Hawaii .* A.B. Morse Co., Printers.

Hawkins, R. A. (2009, January). The Cooperative Marketing of Hawaiian Canned Pineapple, 1908-39. *University of Wolverhampton.*

A Guide to Port Hawaii(). http://file:///D:/The%20pineapple%20project/A-Guide-To-Port-Hawaii.pdf

Greer, R. A. (1998). Along the Old Honolulu Waterfront. *Hawaiian Journal of History, 31*().

Nellist, G. F. (1925, Month Day). The Story of Hawaii and Its Builders. Honolulu Star Bulletin, Ltd.

MacLennan, C. A. (2014). Sovereign Sugar: Industry and Environment in Hawai`i. *University of Hawai`i Press.*

Blunt, & Gresham, (1895, Government Printing Office). Appendix II Foreign Relations of the United States 1894 - Affairs in Hawaii. *House of Representatives. {Ex. Doc. J, 3d Session. Part 1.}*, (17).

Canned Pineapple and Pineapple Juice: Workers of Hawaiian Fruit Packers, Ltd., . (1973, June). Report to the President on Investigation No. TEA-W-194 Under Section 301(c)(2) of the Trade Expansion Act of 1962. , *TC Publication 581.*

Mak, J. (2015, February). Creating "Paradise of the Pacific": How Tourism Began in Hawaii. *University of Hawaii Economic Research Organization.*

Pemberton, C. E. (1964, December). Highlights In The History Of Entomology In Hawaii 1778-1963 . *Hawaiian Sugar Planters' Association*, p. 689-729.

(2014, February). Pineapple in Hawaii - The Early Years. *Newsletter of the Hawai'i Bromeliad Society* , 37(2).

Hawaii to lose its last pineapple cannery (2007). https://www.deseretnews.com/article/660217421/Hawaii -to-lose-its-last-pineapple-cannery.html

Cooper, J. (2012). *Hawaiiâ€™s Top 10 Largest Landowners.* https://www.sfgate.com/hawaii/alohafriday/article/ Hawaii-s-top-10-largest-landowners-3671077.php

Meritt, F. (1914). How We Serve Hawaiian Canned Pineapple. *Hawaiian Pineapple Packers Association, 2nd Edition.*

Fox, C. T. (2017, September). Hawaii's Rainbow of Cultures and How They Got to the Islands. *Honolulu Magazine,* (), . https://www.hawaiimagazine.com/content/hawaiis-rainbow-cultures-and-how-they-got-islands

Hawaii Labor History. (Center for Labor Education & Research). *University of Hawai'i - West O'ahu.* https://www.hawaii.edu/uhwo/clear/home/HawaiiLaborHistory.html

Nakamura, K. (2015). Issei Women and Work: Washerwomen, Prostitutes, Midwives, and Barbers. *The Hawaiian Journal of History, 49.*

Hawkins, R. A. (2007). James D. Dole and the 1932 Failure of the Hawaiian Pineapple Company. *The Hawaiian Journal of History, 41.*

Hori, J. (1981). Japanese Prostitution in Hawaii During the Immigration Period. *Hawaiian Journal of History, 15.*

Hunnewell, J. (1880). *Journal of the Voyage of the "Missionary Packet," Boston to Honolulu 1826.* Charlestown.

Siddall, J. W. (1917). *Men of Hawaii.* Honolulu Star-Bulletin, Limited.

Bartholomew, D. P., Rohrbach, K. G., & Evans, D. O. (2002). Pineapple Cultivation in Hawaii - Overview of Commercial Production Practices. *Cooperative Extension Service College of Tropical Agriculture and Human Resources University ot Hawai'i at Manoa, 31.*

Caswell, E. P., & Apt, W. J. (1989, April). Pineapple Nematode Research in Hawaii: Past, Present, and Future. *Journal of Nematology , 21(2).*

Wilcox, E. V., & Higgins, J. E. (1912, June). The Pineapple in Hawaii. *Hawaii Agricultural Experiment Station, Press Bulletin (36).*

Vandercook, C. (2018, February 7). Remembering the Reality of Plantation Life. . https://www.hawaiipublicradio.org/post/remembering-reality-plantation-life#stream/0

Simone, A. (2015, January 28). For A Group Of Siberians, Hawaii Was Far From A Tropical Paradise . *The World in Words*. https://www.pri.org/stories/2015-01-28/group-siberians-hawaii-was-far-being-tropical-paradise

Varner, N. Strikers, Scabs, and Sugar Mongers - How Immigrant Labor Struggles Shaped the Hawaii We Know Today. . https://www.jacobinmag.com/2017/08/hawaii-labor-history-sugarcane-industry
(2015, August 4). The Camarinos Brothers Picked Hawaii. *The National Herald*. https://www.thenationalherald.com/93430/camarinos-brothers-picked-hawaii/

Theroux, J. (2010, March). The Largest Pineapple in the World. *Honolulu Magazine*, (), . http://www.honolulumagazine.com/core/pagetools.php?pageid=7344&url=%2FHonolulu-Magazine%2FMarch-2010%2FThe-Largest-Pineapple-in-the-World%2F&mode=print

Hawkins, R. A. (1989) The Pineapple Canning Industry During the World Depression of the 1930s, Business History, 31:4, 48-66, DOI: 10.1080/00076798900000084

Ruppenthal, S. (2015, March 25). The Sweet and Sour History of Pineapple in Hawaiʻi. . https://fluxhawaii.com/the-sweet-and-sour-history-of-pineapple-in-hawaii/

Cain, A. (2017, April 25). When Georgia O'Keeffe Went to Hawaii to Paint Pineapples. *Honolulu Museum of Art*.

Aquino, B. A. (2005, December). Why did Filipinos come to Hawaii? -Many Were Lured By False Promises Of Plantation Work. *Star-Bulletin*, 10(345), . http://archives.starbulletin.com/2005/12/11/editorial/special.html

The Anatomy of Ananas comosus . . .
that "Excellent Fruit"— PINEAPPLE

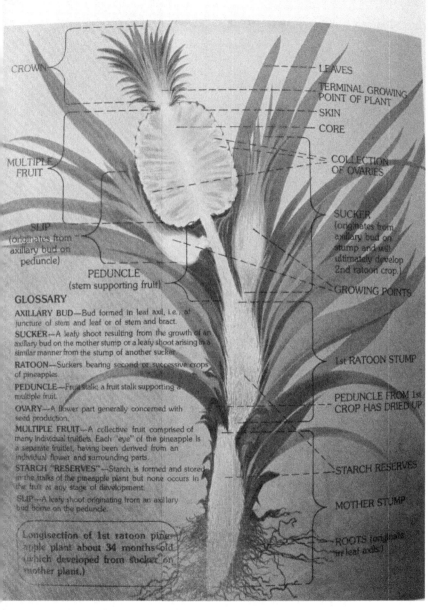

CROWN

LEAVES

TERMINAL GROWING POINT OF PLANT

SKIN

CORE

COLLECTION OF OVARIES

MULTIPLE FRUIT

SUCKER
(originates from axillary bud on stump and will ultimately develop 2nd ratoon crop.)

SLIP
(originates from axillary bud on peduncle)

PEDUNCLE
(stem supporting fruit)

GROWING POINTS

1st RATOON STUMP

PEDUNCLE FROM 1st CROP HAS DRIED UP

STARCH RESERVES

MOTHER STUMP

ROOTS (originate in leaf axils)

GLOSSARY

AXILLARY BUD—Bud formed in leaf axil, i.e., at juncture of stem and leaf or of stem and bract.

SUCKER—A leafy shoot resulting from the growth of an axillary bud on the mother stump or a leafy shoot arising in a similar manner from the stump of another sucker.

RATOON—Suckers bearing second or successive crops of pineapples.

PEDUNCLE—Fruit stalk; a fruit stalk supporting a multiple fruit.

OVARY—A flower part generally concerned with seed production.

MULTIPLE FRUIT—A collective fruit comprised of many individual fruitlets. Each "eye" of the pineapple is a separate fruitlet, having been derived from an individual flower and surrounding parts.

STARCH "RESERVES"—Starch is formed and stored in the stalks of the pineapple plant but none occurs in the fruit at any stage of development.

SLIP—A leafy shoot originating from an axillary bud borne on the peduncle.

Longisection of 1st ratoon pineapple plant about 34 months old (which developed from sucker on mother plant.)

WHAT BECOMES OF A Dōle PINEAPPLE

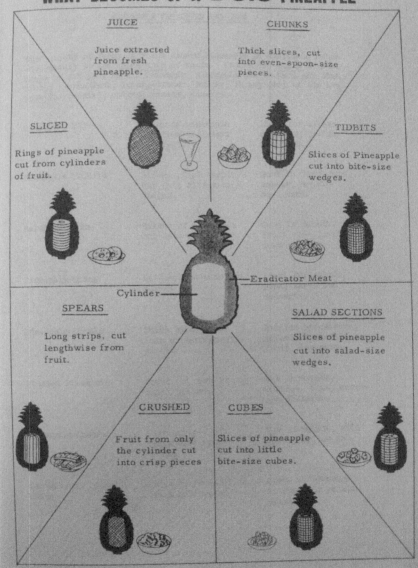

JUICE

Juice extracted from fresh pineapple.

CHUNKS

Thick slices, cut into even-spoon-size pieces.

SLICED

Rings of pineapple cut from cylinders of fruit.

TIDBITS

Slices of Pineapple cut into bite-size wedges.

Eradicator Meat

Cylinder

SPEARS

Long strips, cut lengthwise from fruit.

SALAD SECTIONS

Slices of pineapple cut into salad-size wedges.

CRUSHED

Fruit from only the cylinder cut into crisp pieces

CUBES

Slices of pineapple cut into little bite-size cubes.

Made in the USA
Las Vegas, NV
13 January 2024

84313196R00059